SIJO
Korea's Poetry Form

Edited by Lucy Park and Elizabeth Jorgensen

Sejong Cultural Society

 **PARKYOUNG**

SIJO: Korea's Poetry Form

Edited by Lucy Park, Elizabeth Jorgensen

Produced by PARKYOUNG Press
#210, 53, Gasan digital 2-ro, Geumcheon-gu, Seoul, Republic of Korea
Tel   82-2-733-6771
www.pybook.co.kr
E-mail   pys@pybook.co.kr

Published by Kong & Park USA, Inc.
1440 Renaissance Drive, Suite 430, Park Ridge, IL 60068 USA
www.kongnpark.com

Published Febrary 20, 2022
Printed in Korea

ISBN: 978-1-63519-041-0

Library of Congress Control Number: 2022901961

This book is dedicated to all sijo educators, sijo poets, and sijo lovers.

SIJO: Korea's Poetry Form
Table of Contents

─────────────────────(PART I)─────────────────────

SIJO: Korea's Poetry Form

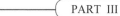

I am grateful to all the living poets and representatives of the poets who gave permission for the translation and publication of modern sijo. I regret that it was impossible to get in touch with appropriate persons in a few cases, although every effort was made.

L.P.

Foreword

David McCann

The Sejong Cultural Society (SCS) in Chicago has played a key role in developing awareness, interest, and involvement in the Korean sijo verse form. Since 2008, the Society has sponsored an annual sijo-writing contest, as well as workshops for teachers to explore ways to bring the sijo into their classrooms. The SCS website provides information, articles, video lectures, performances, and other materials to assist learning about the sijo, writing it and teaching others how to write it.

The present volume brings these resources and more into a single unified set for teachers and writers in Part I and II, followed by an array of sijo poems from the SCS' annual contest.

The contributors to this volume have worked to promote a better understanding of Korean culture and history. I taught Korean literature at Cornell University and Harvard University and turned to writing my own sijo in English relatively recently. My chapter explores sijo's performance dimensions, not only as a verse form that was sung, but also as a dramatically active, engaged form of literary culture.

Linda Sue Park (author of two wonderful collections of sijo poems: *Tap Dancing on the Roof*, with illustrations by Istvan Banyai, and *The One Thing You'd Save*, with illustrations by

Robert Sae-Heng) presents her reflections on her own discovery and writing of sijo.

Dr. Mark Peterson has been involved with numerous international studies programs at Brigham Young University, as Director of the Fulbright Commission in Korea, and with other organizations in Korea and the United States. He sets the Korean sijo alongside the Chinese quatrain, jueju, and Japanese haiku.

Elizabeth Jorgensen has worked with the Sejong Cultural Society in their teacher workshops and other activities. A teacher at Arrowhead Union High School in Wisconsin, her chapters present plans for teaching, editing, and virtual presentation of sijo.

Dr. Lucy Park and the Sejong Cultural Society have organized workshops in Chicago and other cities, involved with not only the Society's sijo projects, but also a wide range of other musical, artistic, and community efforts. Her chapters examine the sijo in contemporary music practice, the range of sijo poets in the contemporary literature scenes in Korea and North America, and the expanding range of the sijo's practice and appeal in languages other than English.

The sijo lesson plans present suggestions from teachers who have worked with students at all levels, from elementary through high school and college.

Part III of this volume comprises a selection of sijo poems chosen from the annual Sejong Cultural Society contests going back to 2008. Delightful in and of themselves as poems, they also provide examples of what it takes to win a sijo contest, and reflections from experts on what they found appealing about the poems.

The contributors to the volume, through a variety of efforts and approaches, share a lively dedication to the recognition and practice of sijo as a Korean verse form having many centuries of history, and to the encouragement of its present and future practice in other languages and cultures.

Let us join the gathering!

PART I

Sijo: Korea's Poetry Form

The Sijo and Performance

David McCann

The sijo is the three-line Korean vernacular verse form, a counterpart to the Japanese haiku. The first line starts the poem, then the second line develops the narrative or the reflection. The third line begins with a twist, a change in perspective, direction, or thought, and then brings the poem to its conclusion. Sijo has a very long and active past, in many dimensions. The tradition continues to the present day with numerous sijo poets, sijo groups and publishers in Korea, as well as an array of translation and publication projects in Korea aimed at expanding the awareness and appreciation of sijo outside of Korea. Programs such as the Sejong Cultural Society's annual writing contest, workshops, and other programs have encouraged the growth of interest in the United States.

The sijo dates back to poets from the thirteenth and fourteenth centuries, but tracing its early history is complicated by the fact that the Korean alphabet, *hangul*, was not developed and promulgated until 1443 under the direction of King Sejong. This means that for sijo predating the alphabet's promulgation, such as those by U Tak (1262-1342) or Jeong Mong-ju (1337-1392), ascription is not certain because no contemporary written accounts can confirm it. Yet sijo very often have stories associated with them about the authors and the circumstances leading to the poem. The stories are told by way of introduction to singing the sijo, whether by a trained performer or by somebody doing a sijo while out on a picnic with some friends in the countryside.

Fourteenth Century

One of the most well-known of all sijo is ascribed to the Goryeo scholar-official and statesman Jeong Mong-ju (1337-1392). As the Yi family patriarch, General Yi Seong-gye, worked to bring down the Goryeo kingdom and set up a new dynasty of his own, he and his followers kept running up against the stubbornly loyal, highly regarded Jeong Mong-ju. The story goes that the fifth son of Yi Seong-gye arranged a banquet, in the course of which he confronted Jeong with a sijo song urging Jeong to relax his vigilant loyalty and to live on and on and on, like the vines on Mansu Mountain. Jeong replied with the following sijo, "Song of a Loyal Heart":

Though this body die and die,
    it may die a hundred times,
my white bones become but dust,
    what's called soul exist or not:
for *my* lord, no piece of this red heart
    would ever change. How could it?

The story goes on that Jeong was murdered by the Yi followers, who correctly understood the poem as a statement of Jeong's loyalty to Goryeo, as Jeong made his way home from the banquet. Yet while there is a stone bridge in North Korea that is said to be the site of Jeong's death, there is no contemporary historical record of the banquet nor any contemporary reference to his sijo. The written record that we do have, *History of the Goryeo*, was compiled a century after. It states that after hearing that Yi Seong-gye had fallen from his horse and was injured, Jeong went to the house to see for himself what condition he was in, and to assess whether he might make some definitive move to stop him. The fifth son, concerned for his father's safety, as soon as Jeong had left the house "... sent Cho Yeong-gyu and five or six others after him. They attacked him on the road and killed him" (McCann 39).

This example can be seen as characteristic of the sijo more generally, as they emerge from a story as a re-presentation of a vivid moment in an individual's or the country's life. Rather than making a single point or drawing a line, sijo exemplify how a poem may be seen as a wave form, even growing out into the dimension of time. Jeong's poem furthermore enacts its own performance as an active examination of the meaning of loyalty as being more than an abstract concept; it takes the reader or listener from outside the person voicing the poem down into the physical body, through the dust of the bones, to the very center, the heart of the being. The poem is a remarkable tour de force.

A great number of Korea's traditional sijo are embedded in similar historical narratives, equally fascinating, and problematic. Still others seem ahistorical in being by or about people who were not part of the ruling *yangban* class. There are, for example, many sijo said to have been composed by *kisaeng* women, members of an entertainment profession somewhat like the Japanese geisha. The most famous of all was Hwang Chini, a sixteenth-century author with a reputation for beauty and artistic accomplishments, as well as a singularly independent mind and will. She composed a half dozen truly remarkable sijo and a number of poems in classical Chinese. There was a Hwang Chini boom in Korea a few years ago, with a novel about her published in North Korea in 2002 winning the South Korean Manhae Prize, another novel published in South Korea in 2004, a TV series in 2006, and other popular cultural representations of her life and work. The trouble, once again, is that the historical record is scanty (see note 1).

Though two or three of Hwang Chini's sijo compete for the greatest esteem, I find the one below, from *Sijo Munhak Sajeon* #1409, intriguing both for its poignant subject as well as its technical accomplishment.

Oh no! What have I done?
    Didn't I know what it was to yearn?
If I'd said, *You must stay,*
    could he have gone? And yet on purpose
I sent him, and now what longing is,
    I realize, I never knew.

translated by David McCann

Of the two most notable features of this poem, one remains lamentably invisible in the English translation, and try as I have, I cannot seem to discover any way at all to register it. The diction of the poem is entirely and purely Korean-language, with the single exception of the word *jeong*, longing feeling. That the vast majority of sijo share with the Korean language itself a fairly broad deployment of Sino-Korean, Chinese-origin terms, is not surprising. It is a characteristic feature of the Korean language. Especially those sijo from the sixteenth and seventeenth centuries reflect a mixed Korean and Sino-Korean vocabulary, while those from the later centuries, perhaps reflecting a popularization of the form and practice, demonstrate a drift away from the Sino-Korean. But here with Hwang Chini's sijo we have an expression of strong, direct feeling pouring forth in nearly pure Korean up to where she points, as Jeong Mong-ju did in his poem: "There, that longing feeling: I never really knew what it was."

The other technical accomplishment of the poem is its deft use of enjambment, the run-on line at the end of line two. Sijo come to a grammatical ending with the line ends, but in Hwang Chini's poem the sense rushes past the usual sentence or clause ending form, through the continuative form deliberately (구태여, *gutaeyeo*), into the twist at the beginning of line three with "sent him away."

Sijo seem to have served upper-class composers and their friends, political enemies, or consorts for a long interval, but the histories take note of a shift in the seventeenth and eighteenth centuries toward popularization of themes, broader popular production—though in the anthologies, sijo likely by commoners are the ones labeled as anonymous—and some shifting toward an expanded, i.e. less rigorous form known as the *sasôl*, or narrative sijo. A number of these later sijo treat sexual themes, perhaps matching a drift in painting toward similar themes and scenes.

Certain of the later, anonymous *sasôl* sijo display wicked, dead-pan humor. One of my favorite examples, which I first encountered in Richard Rutt's book *The Bamboo Grove: An Introduction to Sijo*, presents an exchange between a young wife and her mother-in-law. This sijo (my translation) spins a double twist on the legendarily testy relationship in Korea between wives and their severely proper mothers-in-law.

Oh what am I to do, what am I to do?
    Reverend Mother-in-Law, Oh, what am I to do?
Serving my secret lover his rice, I broke the handle on the brass rice server,
    so now what am I to do, Reverend Mother-in-Law?
Oh dear child, don't worry so. When I was young,
    I broke it many times too.

TWENTIETH CENTURY

Finding a contemporary mode for the sijo in Korea (and in Korean) has been a challenge. Does a change in the line arrangement, an orthographic realignment, make the genre modern? A shift to deliberately chosen modern subjects or images? Other tactics? Or does the sijo simply not lend itself to modernity?

Many theories and practices were tried in the first half of the twentieth century. In North Korea now, the sijo is denigrated for its historic identity as an upper-class literary pursuit. This disapproval seems to miss the significance of the sijo's vernacular Korean linguistic base, as against the literary Chinese expression that was in fact always a marker of ruling class records and communications, as well as literary works. In the South, the sijo continues to have its practitioners, of all generations. But this question still haunts the practice: Can this be a modern, contemporary verse form?

Yi Pyong-gi (1891-1968) remains one of the most highly regarded twentieth century sijo poets. A professor at Seoul National University, he published hundreds of sijo, and in 1932 an essay in the *Tonga Daily* calling for a revival of the sijo, where among other things he urged modern sijo poets to write about contemporary subjects, and to take the additional step of attaching titles. One of his most beloved sijo is in a series called "Orchid." Let the reader try to detect what it is that makes this sijo, first in the sequence of four, modern.

In one hand holding a book
    drowsing away, then suddenly awake;
the bright sun arcs overhead,
    a cool wind rises.
The orchid, two or three buds
    have opened up, full and wide. (see note 2)

The poet Oh Se-young, former President of the Korean Poets Association, published the next example in *Munhak-namu* in the summer of 2004. The reader should have no trouble discerning its modern element.

The cell phone that was resting
    nicely atop the letters case
suddenly shakes its body,
    trembling and quivering.
Even things, when there's nothing to say,
    can feel so—*exasperated!*

INTO THE TWENTY-FIRST CENTURY

In Korea, the Sijo Poets Association is host to a very broad and energized array of meetings, translation and publication efforts, as well as international conferences promoting interest and involvement in sijo. In the last several years, the Association and affiliated publishers have been translating and publishing a lively range of contemporary Korean sijo. Dongkyeong Publishers have published five collections of sijo translations. The Korean Writers Association has two collections, both translated into English, Japanese, and Chinese. Goyo Achim publisher has published two collections of sijo by Kim Min-jeong, *Someone Is Sitting*, and *Going Together*, which present the original sijo poems, strong and clear translations, and photographic images of the scholar stones that comprise the subjects of each poem. Altoran is the publisher of *Sunrise* anthology, a gathering of works by 303 sijo poets, with the original and English translation on each page. The first three poems in the collection are by former presidents of the Republic of Korea, Lee Seung-man, Park Jeong-hee, and Kim Dae-jung.

Here is one of Kim Min-jeong's poems, with the accompanying photograph of its stone subject.

A Masked Angel

Darkness gathers around us,
    hesitantly flinching away.
As viruses float in the air,
    it is a war without weapons.
The angel also wears a mask
    to protect us from viruses.

In the United States, the Sejong Cultural Society (SCS) of Chicago has for many years hosted their annual sijo-writing contest. Originally open for high school students, the contest has expanded now to include any and all contestants in either the pre-college or adult division. SCS has also presented over the years a large number of teacher workshops on sijo, as well as concerts, and other sijo-focused events. The website contains a wide range of information about the sijo form and practice. This book is a part of their efforts.

Azalea: Journal of Korean Literature and Culture is now entering its fourteenth year. *Azalea* has published several special features on the sijo. Volume Two, in 2008, contained the first version of this essay, "Korean Literature and Performance? Sijo!". Volumes Four, Six, Eight and Ten present a range of essays and sijo poems, including winning entries from the Sejong Cultural Society's annual contest.

Sijo journal of poetry and song has published translations, original sijo poems in English, as well as a broad and quite striking array of visual representations of the sijo and its dynamic features.

In 2016, Columbia University Press published *For Nirvana, 108 Sijo Zen Poems* by the poet-monk Cho Oh-hyun, translated by Heinz Insu Fenkl.

Bo-Leaf Books published a gathering of my own sijo, *Urban Temple*, in 2010, which was translated and published in a dual-language edition by Changbi Publishers in Seoul in 2012, a twist in the sijo's unfolding. I'll close this excursion with one of them.

One for Ann

Like a squirrel digging nuts up
    or those crows turning dead leaves
over, I go places and take
    poems, this one from the back seat
of the cab on its way to the airport.
    When I get home, it's all yours.

Notes

1. Four and a half decades ago, during my graduate studies, my advisor Professor Edward Wagner called me into his office to share with me a reference he discovered in an official's collected writings, or *munjip*. Though it was only a brief mention of the famous beauty Hwang Chini, it was dated to the sixteenth century and therefore a confirmation of her existence and reputation at the time. Unfortunately, I do not have the information now.

2. The word *book*, in Korean *ch'aek*, is the term for the published item bought in a store, which prompts an image of a modern reader rather than a scholar seated at a low desk reading a manuscript of some kind. There are a number of traditional, pre-twentieth-century sijo that use the rhetorical turn from "in one hand holding..." to "and in the other..." Often describing a confrontation with some sort of life crisis, such sijo still treat the situation with humor. See, for example, U Tak's (1263-1342) "In one hand holding brambles, with the other grasping a big stick,/ I tried to block the old road with brambles and chase white hairs off with a stick,/ but white hairs knew my intent and came on by the furrowed road instead" (McCann 48).

Works Cited

Kim, Min-jeong. *Going Together*. Goyoachim Publishers, 2020, p227.

McCann, David, ed. *Early Korean Literature: Selections and Introductions*. Columbia University Press, 2000.

McCann, David. *Urban Temple*. Bo-Leaf Books, 2008. Seoul, Changbi Publishers 2012.

Munhak-namu. Summer 2004.

Rutt, Richard, ed. *The Bamboo Grove: An Introduction to Sijo*. Ann Arbor Paperbacks, 1998.

Sijo Munhak Sajeon #1409, p332.

Korean Sijo, Chinese Jueju, and Japanese Haiku

Mark Peterson

Cultures are prone to liking a short poetic form. In English, one thinks of the limerick or perhaps a short quatrain of the "roses are red, violets are blue" variety. Whereas these forms in English are mostly comical, in other countries the short form can be quite serious.

In Chinese, the short form is the jueju, a quatrain—four lines with five beats, sometimes seven beats, per line. The form emerged in the Tang dynasty (618-907) and is often referred to as Tang poetry. Unlike the English short form, the jueju was taken seriously. Topics included nature, love, politics, and drinking, as well as others. And English speakers will welcome the fact that there is end-of-line rhyming (that you don't have with Japanese and Korean poems).

In Japanese, the favorite short-form is the haiku. The haiku has three lines with an exact meter of five beats, seven, and five per line. Topics are most often centered on nature—seasons, trees, frogs, and ponds. The three lines have a structure beyond the meter—the first line sets up the topic, the second line takes the reader in a particular direction, and the third line offers a twist or a resolution, sometimes quite unexpected.

The thing that is most impressive about haiku is not that it is written in Japan, but that the form has taken root in America. As I have been teaching at the university level for over thirty years, whenever I've surveyed classes on their familiarity with haiku, seldom have I found students who have not studied, even written, haiku. The very few who have not studied haiku in school before the university, have mostly been students who were home-schooled. I've heard more recently that home-school curricula are now including haiku. At this point I can say that close to one hundred percent of primary or secondary students have studied and written haiku in America.

Early on in my teaching career, when I asked students if they had written haiku, the responses were that they had studied haiku in high school. In more recent years, I find that students are studying haiku in grade school—mostly the third and fourth grade. Haiku has taken root in America.

Korean sijo is also three lines, like haiku, although it was inspired by the Chinese form. There was no inspiration from haiku—sijo began in the mid-fourteenth century, haiku did not take form until the seventeenth century.

The beauty of haiku is its brevity—squeezing meaning and images into seventeen syllables. The beauty of sijo is also its brevity but in forty-five syllables it can, and does, capture a greater range of ideas and images. There is some confusion about the length of the sijo; it's counted in meter, beats per line. There are web sites that state a sijo should be between forty-five and forty-six beats. While that is generally accurate, there is room for a little more flexibility, maybe between forty-three and forty-eight beats.

Because the sijo is longer than the haiku, it has more options, and in fact, in its natural setting in Korean, does cover a wider range of topics. In English, we are seeing even a greater diversity of topics covered by the sijo.

As for internationalization, haiku has long since arrived. Sijo is well on its way. Jueju gets lost in an already-existing English quatrain. But the jueju achieved an East Asian internationalization centuries before—Korean and Japanese poets read and wrote Chinese poetry before the development of sijo and haiku. Chinese was the *lingua franca* of East Asia in much the same way that Latin was the *lingua franca* of Europe. And Chinese poetic forms were part of the Chinese language influence in Korea and Japan. The Chinese influence was much stronger in Korea than in Japan —Korea, linguistically, became part of the Chinese world to a greater degree than Japan, but Japan bought into Chinese scholarship and culture to a significant degree.

Looking at names reveals the degree of buying into Chinese culture. Korean names are culturally, linguistically, Chinese. Period. Japanese names use Chinese characters, but pronounce the characters in a non-Chinese, indigenous Japanese way. However, there is one big exception—some Japanese names use Chinese pronunciations. An example: I once met a Japanese man who was visiting my school. In typical Japanese fashion, he gave me his name card. I was pleased that I knew how to pronounce his name in Japanese fashion—the Chinese characters were 東山— east mountain—and I knew that east in Japanese was *higashi* and mountain was *yama*. So, I was happy to call him "Higashiyama, sensei."

He seemed pleased and nodded to me, and we talked a bit, and I practiced my limited Japanese. Then he said in perfect English, "I must tell you. I don't pronounce my name 'Higashiyama.' I pronounce it 'Tōsan.'"

"Tōsan" is the Chinese pronunciation—like "tongshan" in Chinese. It would come out "dongsan" in Korean.

I checked on this unusual idea of using the Chinese pronunciation with my Japanese literature professor friends. They explained that among the Japanese population there is a minority group that not only prefer Chinese pronunciation of their names, but are also given to other aspects of Chinese culture. There are some sectors of Japanese society that have been more interested in Confucianism, too—I assume there is a link between these two groups. And I assume Japanese scholarship has included a study of Chinese poetry.

I have more concrete examples of Koreans using Chinese poetry. One of the earliest poems in Korean history was a poem in Chinese on the occasion of the Sui dynasty invasion of Goguryeo. The Korean general, Eulji Mundeok, for whom a street is named in downtown Seoul, wrote a poem to the invading Chinese general.

Your military skills are unparalleled.
They take in all the terrain.
Since you have enjoyed great success.
I hope you now retreat and return home.

How does that poem strike you? If you were the Chinese general, would you pack up and go home? No! You would know you have your enemy on the ropes and you would go after him more vigorously, wouldn't you? Well, that's what the Chinese general did. Do you see a trap about to spring? Yes, General Eulji Mundeok had dammed up the river the Chinese were about to cross. River fordings are among the most dangerous maneuvers for armies—soldiers are vulnerable crossing rivers. As the Chinese pressed forward with their plan to attack, they began fording the river only to find that the Koreans broke the dam, flooding the river valley below and trapping the Chinese armies. The Korean armies descended on them and saw a great victory. The record says of 300,000 soldiers, only 2,970 survived to return to China.

Whereas the account of the deaths is probably an exaggeration, the core story is true. The Koreans had a great victory and the poem, using reverse psychology, urged the Chinese forward into the trap. Aside from the military history related in this story, there is the indication that Korea, in this early time, had scholars, and even generals, who could write Chinese well enough to compose poetry (see Editor's note on page 24).

Indeed, Koreans from the earliest written history were composing Chinese poetry. And the short poem was the ideal. Korea developed its own short form in this early period, the Three Kingdoms period of Korea—a form called the *Hyang-ga* (향가, 鄕歌: countryside song). The Chinese characters for this genre mean the *-ga* (song) of the *hyang* (countryside). The term *hyang* is used in Korea to imply outside-of-the-capital—the rural areas of Korea. But a more likely gloss on the term is that *hyang* meant the area outside of China—thus, Korean songs. These songs were written in Korean. Not in the Korean alphabet—that would not be invented for another 700 years—but in the method of writing Korean words using Chinese in a non-Chinese way. The script was called *idu* and combined Korean pronunciation and Chinese ideas in a way that was complete nonsense to the Chinese reader—though written all in Chinese characters—but the Korean could read it in a Korean way that made sense in the Korean language and thus these songs were Korean songs.

Later in the Goryeo period (918-1392), Koreans developed more literature, songs, and poetry, using Chinese characters in a Korean way. Finally, with the invention of the Korean alphabet, *hangul*, Korea could write its own literature without the cumbersome Chinese script. It was around this time that the sijo emerged. The first sijo were composed before the alphabet was proclaimed, but with the alphabet, there was a new birth of freedom for the Korean poet.

Sijo emerged as a three-line poem with four distinct segments in each line. Sometimes, these three longish lines can be expressed as six shorter lines—but if there are five lines or four lines, it's not a sijo.

In ancient Korea, sijo was sung. The meter was strict, but there was a little flexibility. So, if the writer's work did not fit the prescribed meter, something was wrong. But because of the formula, sijo all came out within the parameters of the desired meter.

As with General Eulji Mundeok's Chinese poem, there have

been sijo written to capture the moment of subsequent historical events. At the fall of the Goryeo dynasty, a general of the Goryeo court was sent off to fight the Chinese, a battle he thought futile and ill-advised. But he was sent off on the mission, to march to China with his men and face sure suicide. He figured he was sent to get him off the scene, and his enemies were behind the assignment. So, on crossing the river into China, they stopped on an island, Wihwado, and the fate of Korea changed forever. He decided to march back to the capital and take over the government, and create a new dynasty. He elicited the help of some who had served the old court and many of those saw the writing on the wall and turned to support the new king-to-be. But not one man. His name was Jeong Mong-ju, and when asked to support the new king, he said, "There are not two suns in the heavens; there cannot be two kings on the throne." In refusing, he knew his fate was death. He wrote one of the most famous sijo of all time.

Though I die, and die again; though I die one hundred deaths.
After my bones have turned to dust, whether my soul lives on or not,
My red heart!, forever loyal to my king, will never fade away.

And they killed him. But he spoke the truth—his heart of pure loyalty has not faded away. Every Korean school child learns that poem. Jeong Mong-ju is alive in every school in Korea today. He is alive in the heart of every Korean soldier who learns of loyalty in his service. And he is alive in the heart of every Korean, because all Koreans can recite that poem with ease. Jeong Mong-ju is alive in that poem.

Loyalty, politics, and serious matters can be covered in sijo. But perhaps the largest category of sijo are love poems. Loyalty and love are related concepts after all.

The most famous poet of love poems was Hwang Chini, a *kisaeng* of the sixteenth century. She could also write Chinese poems, but her most famous work was in the genre of sijo. As a *kisaeng*, she was a servant, in this case, to Gaeseong, the former capital. She had the duty to entertain, sing, dance, and perform poetry for the noblemen who would visit Gaeseong. One particular nobleman was assigned to be the magistrate of Gaeseong, and like all the other magistrates that had come and gone, she expected him to come by and visit. He, on the other hand, was an upright man who was loyal—there it is again—loyal, to his wife back home. Hwang Chini wanted to entice him to change his mind and come visit. She wrote him a poem. To understand the poem, the reader needs to know that her pen name was Bright Moon and his pen name was Jade-green Stream. The Green Hills was a common reference to Korea.

Jade-green Stream, flowing through the Green Hills
    don't be so proud of your easy going.
Once you reach the vast sea,
    to return again will be most difficult.
While Bright Moon fills the empty hills,
    Why not rest a bit, before you go on.

Oh my! When the poem was delivered to him, he was riding his horse fording a stream. He was given the message with the poem while in the middle of the stream, it is said. He was so struck by the power of the poem, that he fell off his horse.

Is the story true? It doesn't matter. The telling of the story is worth the price of admission and sets up the power of the poem. The poem has unseen power in the script and word choice as well—it turns out that the first half of each line is couched in Chinese terms, and the second half of each line is pure Korean. She is saying, within the structure of the poem, that she understands the formal, Chinese, well-educated, bureaucratic, aspect of *his* life; but she is offering the informal, pure Korean, unofficial, intimacy of the poetry. Indeed, in pure Korean, the *hangul* script was sometimes called "women's script". So, by the very structure of the poem she is pulling him off his horse, his high horse, and offering a kind of feminine intimacy one could not get in the government office, on official duties.

Sijo had its heyday in the Joseon period (1392-1910), and unfortunately some people in Korea refer to the sijo as an ancient and dead art. But it is far from dead. There are poetry associations today that foster the writing of sijo in Korea. It is mostly true, sadly, that Korean schools do not teach the writing of sijo as a creative exercise for students today. They are often stuck memorizing the masterpieces and leaving it at that. It's great to memorize the masters—but students should use that knowledge as a template for going forward in creative work and write their own sijo.

The haiku developed later, but gained a foothold in Japanese literature, and perhaps an even greater foothold in America. More new haiku are written in English than in Japanese, in all likelihood. The masterpieces of haiku are associated with a man named Basho. He and a handful of others pushed the genre forward and showed the power of three short lines with five beats, then seven beats, then five beats. The most famous haiku:

An old silent pond.
Suddenly a frog jumps in.
The sound of the splash.

Well, that won't start any wars, and it won't knock a lover off his horse, and it may not seem earth-shaking at all—but it is. That poem, in its sweet simplicity, says everything about haiku. Short. Full of imagery. Simple. Contemplative. Natural.

Haiku tend to follow that formula—images of nature, sweet, simple, contemplative, and highly structured. The most important thing, to me, about haiku, is that haiku has become a part of American culture. Haiku is taught in grade school and children not only learn about a frog jumping into the pond, but they write their own haiku—that is the key. American haiku have themes of nature, like Japanese haiku, but they go beyond that and cover an infinite variety of topics. Haiku has become a part of American culture.

My favorite example of a haiku with a theme in American culture is the following by Ron Loeffler:

Christmas

Glass balls, glowing lights
Dead tree in the living room
Killed to honor birth.

This haiku is just perfect—meter, structure, but more than that, it is so opposite of Japanese culture and so quintessentially American in its culture. And it makes us, as Americans, look at ourselves. Yes, we kill a tree to honor the birth of the baby Jesus; and we put the *dead* tree in the *living* room. The contrast in image and content is overpowering.

The three lines of a haiku each have a different purpose—the first, to set up the scene; the second to develop the idea; and the third offers a resolution with something unexpected. Bingo! This haiku does exactly that—first line: you can see a Christmas scene —glass ball ornaments, glowing lights, yes!, it's Christmas. Second line: a little somber, *dead* tree! We think of it as a Christmas tree, but now we see it is *dead*. And where is it? In the *living* room. Well, it's not a *living* room for the dead tree!

And the third line resolves the issue with a punch in the gut— *killed*, the tree was *killed*—and why? To commemorate the birth of the baby of Bethlehem. The irony. Shouldn't we plant a tree? Plant a seed? Hatch an egg? There ought to be a better way to commemorate a birth than killing something?!?!

So, the poem sets up contrasts and makes us look at the familiar in a new and revealing way. It turns Christmas on its head, and helps us to see it in a new light. It's magical.

There are many haiku in English. They look at nature, as do their role models in Japan, but they look at many other items in

American culture as well. Haiku is a part of American culture.

That, frankly, is my dream for sijo in America. I would hope that a poem similar to haiku—structurally, three lines, but a bit more elaborate—would be the next step for American education. It seems a natural fit to me. I'll leave you with a sijo.

All students in the U.S.
    learn haiku in their schools.
Three short lines, regular rhythm;
    five, seven, five beats to the line.
Now sijo needs to be planted in the curriculum.
    It's the next step for us to take.

> ***Editor's note:*** There are two versions of stories on the Battle of Salsu River and how General Eulji Mundeok's small army crushed the invading mighty and numerically superior Chinese army. Also, there are two versions of the Chinese general's response to General Eulji Mundeok's poem. (see page 100)

1. Shin, Chae-ho신채호. Joseon Sang-go-sa (History of Old Joseon) 조선상고사. 1948 (originally published in 1924)
2. Soo-Seo수서, 60 volume (60권 열전). 제25 우중문. No.25 U Joong-moon
3. KIM, Jinwung. TUCKER ABC-CLIO Spencer. KIM, Grace. How did the Weaker Actor Defeat the Stronger Actor? ESJEAS 2018.18.2.005 (https://muse.jhu.edu/article/708027) page 15
4. Great battle of Salsu river 살수대첩, Encyclopedia of Korean Culture한국민족문화대백과사전

Sijo in the USA

Lucy Park

The Sejong Cultural Society was established in Chicago in 2003 by first-generation Korean immigrants. Our mission is to increase awareness of Korean cultural heritage among American youth through music and literature. We started the Sejong Music Competition in 2004 and Sejong Writing Competition in 2006, which initially included only an essay competition.

Two years after beginning our writing competition, our planning committee chair, Professor Heinz Insu Fenkl, asked us if we were interested in adding a sijo competition and introduced us to his friend Professor David McCann at Harvard University. We were surprised at the thought of writing sijo in English. To us, sijo was an esoteric form of poetry, an old cultural remnant only a handful of poets—not lay people—dabbled in; our exposure to sijo was limited to those great poems written by highly respected traditional scholars. It had never occurred to us to attempt writing them ourselves. But after speaking with Professor McCann, who was already teaching sijo to his students at Harvard University, and investigating on the internet, we discovered that sijo had already been enthusiastically embraced by a small community of

American and Canadian poets.

Soon I learned from others that American students were taught various forms of poetry as early as grade school, and that one of the most ubiquitous forms was the Japanese haiku. If one form of Asian poetry could manage such widespread dissemination among Americans, we wondered, why couldn't another?

After further discussion with and encouragement from Professors McCann and Fenkl, in 2008 we launched the sijo category of our writing competition in collaboration with the Korea Institute at Harvard University. As we launched the sijo competition, we posted materials on how to write and teach sijo on our website. Then we embarked on an expansion of educational programs for American educators on how to teach sijo in their classrooms. Our competition asked students to write a single sijo in English on any subject, and it quickly became a success: our second year saw nearly triple our first year's entries, and the numbers continued to increase from there, up to thirteen hundred sijo from forty-one states in 2014.

During the first several years, we noticed that entire classes of students were submitting entries together—in other words, teachers were using our competition in their curricula, much to our surprise and delight. This fulfilled our main goal of seeing sijo taught in classrooms, and we began looking for ways to expand. At the same time, we started to notice certain teachers who were regulars in our competition submitting sijo from three or four, to as many as one hundred, students year after year, and we reached out to them for collaboration.

After securing a grant from the Seoul-based Korea Foundation, our first project was a two-day, three-part event in 2010. The first day consisted of a sijo workshop intended mainly for educators, where we were able to finally meet our competition's regulars in addition to other college and high school English teachers. Newcomers had the opportunity to write and learn about sijo and its history, and, given our primary goal of assisting teachers in introducing sijo to their classes, discussions were held during which teachers could suggest and exchange ideas on their methods.

The first event of the second day was devoted to a lecture by Professor McCann at the Chicago Public Library. Though open to and attended by various interested members of the public, our main goal was to begin creating our own sijo-related resources—in this case, a video series of Professor McCann's lectures. We have since expanded our resource collection with a series of lectures by Professor Mark Peterson of Brigham Young University, another champion of and lecturer on sijo. We have also continued to organize similar lectures for the public over the years, including several events at the Poetry Foundation in Chicago.

The second event of the second day was for the general public. Held at a Korean-run, Asian-focused art gallery in the heart of Chicago, the event was part poetry reading, part concert, art viewing, and wine tasting, but all with a Korean twist. Sijo were read by Professor McCann and Korean television producer Won Jung Park; Korean musicians performed traditional music; the refreshments included *soju* and *makkgeoli*, Korean liquor. While the workshop was intended for educators and the library lecture for the general public, here we sought to draw the attention of fine arts enthusiasts who would be more enticed by a poetry reading amid art and wine, than a lengthy lecture. Incidentally, a handful of graduate students and teachers were among our attendees.

After an enthusiastic response from our participants, the workshop became an annual staple of our program with several dozen participants from across the country, many of whom went on to send their students' work to our competition. We have also begun to present a condensed form of the workshop at a number of Korean-themed seminars for American educators across the country, including events in Los Angeles, Seattle, Dallas, and Atlanta. We have collaborated with the National Korean Studies Seminar (formerly known as Korean Academy for Educators) since 2011 at their annual week-long seminar at the Los Angeles Korean Cultural Center.

While the two-day workshop provided a foundation, our range of projects and presenters is much wider today. Many of our regular teacher participants now collaborate with us, spreading sijo in the USA through published articles, lesson plans, and recorded lectures.

During this time, Mr. Duane Johansen, a high school English teacher from Indiana, sent us this remark:

> Brandon was a student in my creative writing class the first semester of this school year. Coming into the class, Brandon didn't consider himself a significantly accomplished writer and certainly not a good poet. As he said, "I hated poetry. I didn't understand it and didn't take the time to learn how to comprehend it." He was, after all, a good-ole-boy: a starter on the football team and an avid outdoorsman. However, when we started the poetry unit, Brandon started to show some promise. He really started to shine when we wrote sijo. Each student only had to write one, but Brandon wrote three (all about hunting or fishing, his favorite topics: the cover of his final project for my class has a picture of him on a turkey hunt). Again, in his words: "We began writing a type of poem called sijo, and I wrote some really good sijos. [This] improved my writing a lot. I started writing with more detail and depth. It also made me realize I could do things that I never would have done before." I asked Brandon if I could enter one of his sijo in the contest, and he agreed, although this was clearly out of his comfort zone. I hope he does well in the contest, but even if doesn't, I'm proud that he's started to see himself in a way that he never did before.

This is Brandon's sijo:

A Buck Trots Through the Woods

A buck trots through the woods, looking for a couple of does.
In the distance, he sees a pair playing; he gets into a full run.
A coyote leaps toward the buck; his antlers pierce the heart of the coyote.

This, and other strikingly similar statements from teachers and students across the country, was truly inspiring. Brandon's sijo didn't win, but in our eyes, this was a far greater accomplishment —not only was an American high school student learning about the sijo in his English class, but in doing so, he gained interest and confidence in his writing. We could not have hoped for a better outcome, and we made the decision to move the majority of our organization's efforts into developing our sijo projects.

It was also at educators' suggestions that we began our video recording project. Many teachers who attended our workshops were curious to see how others with more experience tackled the subject with their students. To that end, we visited the high school classrooms of several of our collaborating teachers and made videos of the classes in which they taught their students about sijo. These videos of sijo classes in Virginia, Wisconsin, Tennessee, and Colorado, can be seen on our YouTube Channel.

To expand on this, we invited Ms. Elizabeth Jorgensen, a Wisconsin-based high school English teacher whose class had already been featured in one of our videos, to teach a group of selected third- and fourth-grade students. By the end of her one-hour-long class, the students were writing sijo on their own and finger-counting their syllables as they worked.

We started reaching out to mainstream events for English teachers and writers. Professor McCann and Ms. Jorgensen have presented for the past several years at the National Council for Teachers of English (NCTE), the largest organization of English teachers of North America, on teaching sijo in high school.

Jorgensen also presented on sijo instruction at annual meetings of the Wisconsin State Reading Association, Ohio Council of Teachers of English, Illinois Reading Council, and Wisconsin Writers Association. In addition, Jorgensen published multiple articles on teaching sijo in English teacher journals, including *Ohio Journal of English Language Arts*, *Wisconsin State Reading Association Journal*, and *Edutopia* (by the George Lucas Educational Foundation). In 2020, due to the coronavirus pandemic, NCTE's annual meeting was conducted via Zoom. Ms. Jorgensen's presentation on teaching sijo was featured in one of the interactive workshops.

Our largest ongoing project is something in a different vein and intended for younger generations. Initially, sijo were first and foremost written as songs and performed with musical accompaniment; with that in mind, we wanted to explore how we could bridge the gap between traditional poetry form and contemporary mainstream pop music. For this, we began to work with Elephant Rebellion (ER), a Chicago-based community-oriented artists' collective, and selected hip-hop as our medium. Using a variety of sijo, ranging from traditional classic poems to winners from our competition, and even poems the members themselves wrote, ER uses sijo as a basis for the lyrics of hip-hop compositions. As a group of musicians with highly diverse ethnic backgrounds, many of them first generation immigrants and minorities, ER jumped at the chance to use twelfth-grader Roberto Santos' 2013 first place sijo:

Still American

They say go, return to land that I don't know. It makes no sense.
Born and raised American, so Mexico is still foreign.
Culture kept, but this is my home. Immigrant, no: Hispanic.

Our recent projects involve sijo and music concerts featuring classical music, hip-hop, and jazz ensembles. Sijo and music is described in more detail in another chapter.

During the coronavirus pandemic, we offered virtual sijo workshops. We've expanded our program for teachers to include an Online Sijo Class, a five-week-long asynchronous program combined with Zoom meetings for discussion and question and answer sessions.

The Sejong Writing Competition is currently going strong with well over one-thousand sijo entries each year—a long way from our first year of 150. Our efforts to reach teachers and students alike are being met with interest and curiosity, and we believe this trend will grow.

In 2020, we added the Wisconsin Sijo Competition. This was a collaborative project with the University of Wisconsin-Madison Center for East Asian Studies. This competition is open to residents of Wisconsin. In 2021, we started the Sejong International Sijo Competition. Over two hundred poets from nineteen countries participated in this inaugural event. This competition is open to all poets regardless of nationality or age.

The sijo has proven itself to be not only an interesting form of poetry but also a window into an often-overlooked culture. Given sijo's great accessibility to newcomers and value for creative writers, we hope that we—and others—are able to fully explore its potential in the coming years, not only among Korean or English speakers, but also among people speaking other languages.

Works Cited

Park, Lucy. Bringing Sijo to a New World. *Azalea: A Journal of Korean Literature and Culture*, University of Hawaii Press. 10:97-103, 2017

This work appears with permission of the Harvard University Korea Institute from YoungJun Lee, *Azalea*: *A Journal of Korean Literature and Culture* Volume 10 (Cambridge, Mass: Harvard University Korea Institute, 2017), © The President and Fellows of Harvard College, 2017.

Contemporary Sijo Poets in Korea and North America

Lucy Park

KOREAN SIJO POETS IN THE TWENTIETH CENTURY

The turn of the twentieth century marked the end of the Joseon dynasty, the last of Korea's dynasties, and the beginning of the Japanese annexation of Korea, which lasted from 1910 until 1945. Among other extreme changes to Koreans' lives, Japan's absolute rule over Korea resulted in aggressive cultural assimilation of the Korean people. Language, widely recognized as a critical element in the formation of national identity, was a focus of both the Japanese government and Korean nationalist efforts. The Japanese enforced a "Cultural Assimilation Policy" in which Korean culture was simply squashed. Koreans were required to speak Japanese and take Japanese names. The Korean media was subject to total control by Japan. The publications of Korean-language books and newspapers were heavily censored or prohibited with the sole exception of a government-owned daily.

Many Korean resisters attempted to counteract cultural annihilation by promoting Korean nationalism and identity in many ways, including through language. In 1908, while Korea was not yet fully annexed but instead named a protectorate of Japan, a group of Korean intellectuals established the Korean Language Society in order to preserve Korean literary and linguistic culture, heritage, and identity. Several prominent poets and linguistic scholars proposed the revival of sijo as a national poetry form in a movement to keep a sense of national identity. Choe Nam-seon (1890-1957), a leading member of the Korean independence movement and prominent publisher, historian, and poet, published the first collection of modern Korean sijo in 1926. The work was titled *One Hundred and Eight Defilements* (백팔번뇌) and focused primarily on lamenting the loss of his country, and his desire for independence. Today Choe is widely credited with pioneering modern Korean poetry.

Choe's efforts to revive classical sijo were met with enthusiasm. Amidst Choe's contemporaries was Yi Pyong-gi (1891-1968), now considered one of the grandfathers of the modern sijo. Yi and other prominent poets proposed modernizing the sijo form, and encouraged writing in multiple stanzas when a single stanza couldn't tell the whole story. Yi also stressed that each sijo in a multi-stanza sijo not stand alone, as in classical forms, but rather meld with other stanzas to create a complete poem.

The end of World War II saw the liberation of Korea in 1945 and a revitalization of interest in modern sijo. Preeminent poets published anthologies of sijo and academic articles on writing sijo, unequivocally establishing the form as a genre of Korean literature. Among other differences, the contents of modern sijo differed from pre-liberation era works, which were closer to the musical genre than literary. The focus of modern sijo shifted to contemporary topics, and a more literary voice emerged from the lyrical styles of old. Modern sijo are more likely to have a title, use a variety of topics, and are frequently written in multiple stanzas (연시조), also known as sijo sequence.

In the years following their liberation, Koreans experienced extraordinary hardships living through the Korean War, then faced censorship and secret police under dictatorships while striving to create a strong democratization movement. The number of sijo poets increased during these turbulent times, and many sijo organizations were formed, including the Korea Sijo Poetry Society, the Korean Sijo Poets' Association, and the Society of Sijo Poets. Such organizations were active in publishing monthly or quarterly journals and organizing seminars and workshops. In addition to Choe Nam-seon and Yi Pyong-gi, notable poets of this era include Yi Un-sang (1903-1982), Kim Sang-ok (1920-2004), and Cho Oh-hyun (1942-2018).

Recently, a new school of sijo poets proposed writing sijo without keeping the three- or six-line structure or syllable count. Many sijo poets refuse to acknowledge sijo that fail to adhere to the basic structure and syllable count established centuries ago. However, writing in multiple stanzas has been well-accepted by the majority of modern sijo poets.

As of 2021, roughly two thousand sijo poets have published sijo in newspapers or professional journals and are registered members of sijo poets' organizations. At least five hundred scholars specialize in the academic study of sijo or are sijo critics. Although sijo is not widely taught to pre-college students, many sijo poets' organizations, individual poets, and pre-college teachers are making the effort to introduce sijo to students. One of the most successful of these organizations is *Children's Sijo World* (어린이 시조나라), a quarterly journal established in 2010 dedicated to publishing sijo written for and by children. The founder, Mr. Seo Kwan-ho, is a sijo poet and educator who has published numerous sijo collections. In 2010, he created a sijo contest in Korea for children sponsored by the Sejong Cultural Society. Mr. Seo's sijo lesson plan is included in this book.

In addition to the *Children's Sijo World* competition, sijo competitions run by poets' organizations or newspapers exist for students as well as adults in Korea. One notable competition is organized by the *Joong-Ang Daily* (중앙일보), one of Korea's four major newspapers. This competition was created in 1981 for adults. In 2013, they added a pre-college division. Approximately one thousand students applied to the competition in 2019 and five hundred advanced to the final round.

Although interest in sijo is smaller in the United States and other western countries than it is in Korea, the Sejong Cultural Society is hoping to spark an interest in English-speaking countries with our English-language sijo competition. Ultimately we hope to see increasing interest among speakers of languages beyond Korean and English.

Contemporary Sijo Poets in Korea

Choe Nam-seon (1890-1957) 최남선

Choe Nam-seon was one of the most influential figures in the history of Korean literature. By successfully publishing some of the first modern magazines in Korea, he promoted the use of *hangul* (Korean alphabet) as a new literary medium and sought to create a style of Korean literature that would be more accessible to ordinary people. As a leading member of the Korean independence movement, he organized nonviolent movements and was one of the major drafters of the Korean Declaration of Independence, for which he was imprisoned by the Japanese government.

Sitting Alone
혼자 앉아서
from *Modern Korean Verse in Sijo Form*, selected and translated by
Jaihiun Kim
The English translation does not follow the standard sijo structure; the original Korean correctly adheres to the standard form.

The silent rain sounds
as it drips from the eaves.
While waiting in vain for someone
who will not come
I rivet my eyes to the closed door
on the chance it may open.

가만히 오는 비가 낙수져 소리하니
오마지 않은 이가 일도 없이 기다리져
열릴듯 닫힌 문으로 눈이 자주 가더라.

Embrace (first and third stanzas)
안겨서 **(1&3연)**

"You" refers to Joseon (Korea) and "winter" is a bleak reality
of a lost country.

1
Because of you the moon shines bright.
The flower flares fair because of you.
In truth, if you were not here
honey would lose its sweetness, wormwood its bitterness.
Because of you a veil is lifted off the world
at the rising of the sun.

3
If I do not
compare you,
I cannot tell for sure
that you are incomparable.
I can but admire
your brightness of being even in deep winter.

님자채 달도 밝고 님으로 해 꽃도 고와
진실로 님 아니면 꿀이 달랴 쑥이 쓰리

해 떠서 번하옵기로 님 탓인가 하노라

무어라 님을 할가 해에다가 비겨 볼가
쓸쓸과 어두움이 얼른하면 쫓기나니
아무리 겨울 깊어도 응달 몰라 좋아라

YI PYONG-GI (1891-1968) 이병기

Yi Pyong-gi is considered one of the fathers of the modern sijo, known for his efforts to preserve and revive the sijo alongside Yi Un-sang. He was a prolific poet and educator and a member of the Korean Academy of Arts; during his life he won numerous literary awards and prizes. In his technical efforts to modernize sijo, he is known for writing works with lengthened verses with an exquisitely refined style.

RAIN 2
비 **2**
from *Modern Korean Verse in Sijo Form*, selected and translated by
Jaihiun Kim

I see you're prepared to leave,
your bags already packed.
The innocent rain has been falling
since early in the morning.
O rain, keep falling till tomorrow
and again tomorrow.

Forget about leaving now, friend,
it's a long way home.
And the rain that keeps falling
till evening
adds to my desire
to make you stay.

The moment you shake
off my hand,
I awake from my dream
only to hear the pleasant rain,
and I close my eyes again,
relieved to see your bags untouched.

짐을 매어놓고 떠나시려 하는 이 날
어두운 새벽부터 시름없이 내리는 비
내일도 내리오소서 연일 두고 오소서

부디 머나먼 길 떠나지 마오시라
날이 저물도록 시름없이 내리는 비
저으기 말리는 정은 나보다도 더하오

잡았던 그 소매를 뿌리치고 떠나신다
갑자기 꿈을 깨니 반가운 빗소리라
매어 둔 짐을 보고는 눈을 도로 감으오

YI UN-SANG (1903-1982) 이은상

Yi Un-sang was a poet, historian, and professor dedicated to
the revival and modernization of sijo alongside Yi Pyong-gi; now,
he is considered a giant in modern Korean literature. A recipient
of the Rose of Sharon National Medal of Honor (1970), many of
his poems were used as lyrics for Korean art songs. He is
particularly known for his lyricism and short, powerful poems,
contrasting with other lengthened styles.

I Will Write a Poem Too
나도 같이 시를 쓴다
from *The Bamboo Grove: An Introduction to Sijo* by Richard Rutt

Up above the shimmering sea
    two or three seagulls are hovering.

Rolling, wheeling, they write a poem.
I do not know the alphabet they use.
On the broad expanse of sky
I will write a poem too.

아득한 바다 위에 갈매기 두엇 날아 돈다.
너훌너훌 시를 쓴다. 모르는 나라 글자다.
널따란 하늘 복판에 나도 같이 시를 쓴다.

YANG SANGGYUNG (1903-1988) 양상경

A poet and educator, Yang published several sijo anthologies. He was head of the Dong Myung School in Nanjing, China, which was dedicated to educating Korean descendants in China. Most of the students were children of Korean independence fighters.

On Sijo Writing
시조작법
from *The Bamboo Grove: An Introduction to Sijo* by Richard Rutt
A note by Richard Rutt: "The first stanza is a careful description of a Korean woman's dress, which consists of a very full skirt and a bodice tied over the right breast with a broad long bow or ribbon. The basic pattern of fours refers to the number of syllables in each phrase" (262).

The first line is a full skirt, the second is the bodice;
On reaching the third and last, the neat collar has been added.
Lightly tie the ribbon bow, and the charm of the dress will appear.

The basic pattern of fours is like the counting of the days:
Twenty-eight will make a month, thirty-one, too, will make a month.
Set the stem, and when leaves and flowers bloom fragrance will come
of itself.

The bright moon lighting up the sky, clear and white above the ground,
Is it just the shining soul of the sijo of ancient masters?
The mere sound of a lute in moonlight, is that not a sijo too?

치마는 초장이요 저고리는 중장인가.
반듯한 동정 달아 말장(末章)이라 이르리니
젖가슴 탐스런 맛도 옷맵시로 풍기네.

사사조(四四調) 기본형(基本形)은 날수와 같은지라.
이십팔(二十八)도 한달이오 삼십일(三十一)도 한달이니
절(節) 맞춰 일 되고 꽃 피면 향기(香氣) 절로 나리라.

높은 하늘 밝은 달이 뚜렷이 걸린 뜻은
옛 님의 시조혼(時調魂)을 받들어 비침일까.
달아래 거문고 소리 시조(時調)런듯 하여라.

CHUNG WAN-YOUNG (1919-2016) 정완영

Chung Wan-young was the editor of a coterie magazine
Paulownia in the 1940s. Later he gained recognition as a sijo
poet when he won literary prizes and his sijo were published in
newspapers in the early 1960s.

Early Spring
초봄
from *Azalea: Journal of Korean Literature and Culture* 2011,
translation by Sunghee Kim

While I wash the window, blowing my breath on it,
A bird flies and wipes the sky clean.
Tomorrow, the magnolia will be out and clean the colors from the
clouds.

내가 입김을 불어 유리창을 닦아내면
새 한 마리 날아가며 하늘을 닦아낸다

내일은 목련꽃 찾아와 구름 빛도 닦으리

CHO OH-HYUN (1938-2018) 조오현

Master Cho Oh-hyun was a Buddhist monk, abbott of Shinheungsa Temple in Sorak mountain. He was regarded as one of the greatest contemporary sijo poets in Korea.

The Sound Of My Own Cry
내 울음소리

from *For Nirvana: 108 Zen Sijo Poems* by Cho Oh-hyun, translation by Heinz Insu Fenkl

Fenkl noted that Master Cho's sijo is a zen poetry:

> Their surface is easy to read and comprehend—very smooth in the source language. Their narrative quality, their allusions, and their use of understood tropes allow one to arrive at an "apparent" poem without requiring deep reflection. They can be appreciated aesthetically on this first pass. But the first pass only reveals a single layer or facet of the poem, which then leaves a kind of resonance—an image, a word, a phrase will linger naggingly in memory, like an echo. This brings one back to the poem to read again and to discover another narrative, theme, or poem in superposition (Cho 108).

In the woods at noon
I hear a bird cry out

On the shore, mid-morning,
I hear the gulls

When will I hear
The sound of my own cry?

한나절은 숲속에서 새 울음소리를 듣고
반나절은 바닷가에서 해조음 소리를 듣습니다
언제쯤 내 울음소리를 내가 듣게 되겠습니까

HAN YONGUN (1879-1944) 한용운

Han Yongun was a distinguished Buddhist monk, poet, and a leader of the Korean Independence movement of 1919. The following poem uses a boy on an ox to express the poet's concern about his nation.

Untitled

from *The Bamboo Grove: An Introduction to Sijo* by Richard Rutt

In the slanting rays of the evening sun
    a boy on an ox plays his flute.
"If your ox bears no burden
    let it carry my worries."
"Taking them is easy enough:
    it's another thing to set them down."

비낀 볕 소등 위에 피리부는 저 아이야
너의 소 짐 없거든 나의 시름 실어주렴
싣기는 어렵잖아도 부릴 곳이 없어라

KIM SANG-OK (1920-2004) 김상옥

Kim is a poet, calligrapher, painter, and author. He published several sijo anthologies. He showed exceptional talent in a variety of literary genres including sijo, poems for children, and essays. He received numerous awards for his achievement in the literary field. Jaihiun Kim, the translator, stated that Kim Sang-ok distinguished himself by his unique use of language and imagery.

The Jade Flute

옥저

from *Modern Korean Verse in Sijo Form,* selected and translated by
Jaihiun Kim

A note by Jaihiun Kim: "The poet relates the master flutist to
the jade flute kept for over a thousand years. The jade flute is
one of the three national treasures of the Shilla kingdom (57
BC-935 AD)" (64).

His eyes gently closed,
his lips moistened,
the flutist moved his fingers
busily over each hole.
His music echoed through the whole kingdom
like the flow of the Milky Way.

The silver sound resonating in the air
holds a millenium of history.
The master musician's breath
still lingers in the flute.
A lonely soul,
how could he have lived otherwise?

지그시 눈을 감고 입술을 축이시며,
뚫린 구멍마다 임의 손이 움직일 때,
그 소리 은하(銀河) 흐르듯 서라벌에 퍼지다.

끝없이 맑은 소리 천년을 머금은 채,
따스히 서린 입김 상기도 남았거니,
차라리 외로울망정 뜻을 달리하리요!

IM JONG-CHAN (1945-) 임종찬

Im Jong-chan is a professor emeritus of Korean Literature at
Busan University. As a prolific sijo writer, he published

numerous anthologies of his sijo poems. He was the past president of the Korean Academy of Sijo, an association of academicians dedicated to studying sijo.

Bleeding Heart
금낭화
from *Potato Flower, sijo collection* by Im Jong-chan, translated by Park Hyang Seon

I'd like to put your countenance
in the pouch of a bleeding heart flower.

When the pouch becomes full,
I will bury it as if it were a seed.

Next spring, your sweet countenance
is sure to bloom as the flower.

금낭화 꽃주머니
그대 얼굴 담으련다

한 가득 담기거든
씨로 익혀 묻을란다

내봄에 그대 얼굴이
금낭화로 필꺼야

SEO KWAN-HO (1948-) 서관호

Seo Kwan-ho, who is based in Busan, Korea, is the founder and publisher of the *Children's Sijo World* (어린이 시조나라). Seo has published seven anthologies of sijo for children and received numerous accolades as a poet, educator, and publisher.

Autumn

가을

from *Sijo Even My Puppies Know* (강아지도 아는 시조) by Seo
Kwan-ho, translated by Lucy Park

Ginko leaves are falling,
settling gently on my shoulders.

This beautiful leaf,
I longed to send it to someone dear.

Sun-yi! I placed the leaf on the pond
where we used to play together.

살포시 어깨위에
은행잎 내려앉고

예쁜 낙엽 한 장
뉘라도 주고 싶다

순이야!
놀던 연못에
나뭇잎 배 띄운다.

Sijo Poets in North America

Korean sijo was introduced to North Americans in the middle
of the twentieth century through articles and books written by a
number of authors, e.g., Peter H. Lee (1964), Inez Kong Pai
(1965), Richard Rutt (1971), David McCann (1977), Jaihiun Kim
(1982), In-Sob Zong (1983), Unsong Kim (1986), Kevin
O'Rourke (1987), and Constantine Contogenis (1997). Since then,
many North American poets have written original English sijo. A
few poets stand out as pioneers in writing English sijo and

spreading it in North America.

DAVID MCCANN

David McCann, the Korea Foundation Professor of Korean Literature, received his B.A. from Amherst College, taught English for two years in Korea in the Peace Corps, and received M.A. and Ph.D. degrees from Harvard. He taught Korean literature at Harvard from 1997 until his retirement in 2014. He has published thirty-one books: anthologies, studies on Korean literary culture, translations of the prominent poets of Korea such as Kim Sowol, Ko Un, Seo Chongju, and many others. His work in the field of Korean literature was recognized by the Manhae Prize in 2004, and the Korean Culture Order of Merit in 2006. McCann has published many poems in such distinguished media as *Poetry, Descant*, and *Ploughshares*. His poem "David" was included in the Pushcart Prize Anthology III. He published ten collections of his poems including *Urban Temple: Sijo, Twisted & Straight* (Bo-Leaf Press, 2010), *Same Bird* (Moon Pie Press, 2016), and *Out of Words* (Moon Pie Press, 2019). These books include a few sijo, many freestyle poems, and a few haiku.

He wrote "First Sijo: A Night in Andong" while stationed in Korea as a member of the Peace Corps. The poem was inspired by his boarding house accomodations in Andong village. His room was close to a pig pen and he often heard pigs grunting as he was entering or leaving. McCann is fluent in Korean and wrote this sijo in English and Korean.

First Sijo: A Night in Andong
from *Urban Temple: Sijo, Twisted and Straight* by David McCann

One night in Andong
    after a tour of back-alley wine shops,

head spinning, I staggered down

the narrow, paddy-field paths,

when the two pigs grunted
    "So, you! Home at last?"

하룻밤 안동 시내 골목술집 구경하고
머리가 삥삥돌때 밭둑길을 거닐다가
도야지 꿀꿀 소리야 이제 왔노 하노라

Untitled

from *Education about Asia,* Vol 15, pp. 53-54, Spring 2010

All through lunch, from my table
    I keep an eye on your disputes,
green lobsters in the bubbling
    tank by the restaurant door.
Slights, fights, bites—Whatever the cause,
    make peace and flee, escape with me!

KIM UNSONG

Kim is a Korean-born poet and scientist. He studied microbiology and molecular biology. He taught and researched in various institutes including NASA Ames Research Center, University of Illinois, and Michigan State University. After retiring from his science career in 1982, he dedicated his effort to writing and translating Korean poetry. He won the first prize from the World Poetry Society International in 1987. He published nine books on Korean and Chinese poetry.

In 1986, Kim Unsong introduced sijo by translating one hundred masterpieces for *Poet,* an international monthly. Ever since, sijo-writing has been blossoming in the Western world. Kim sponsored poetry contests in California, Arizona, and Canada. Kim published his own sijo collection in 1987. He distributed his book widely in the USA and in Europe. Since many of the poems use syllable counts not consistent with sijo, other sijo poets did not embrace his approach.

Silence

from *Poems of Modern Sijo* by Kim Unsong

Impulsive talkers
cover their weaknesses untold

No matter how passionate they talk
their stories can hardly be sold

Silence often overcomes the speech
turning it to gold

LARRY GROSS (1927-2014)

A poet, writer, editor, and educator, Larry Gross earned a doctorate from Florida State University, taught at Tallahassee Community College for twenty years, and became a godfather of English sijo. His poetry, articles, and reviews have appeared in various periodicals in the United States, Canada, England, Korea, Japan, India, Australia, and New Zealand. Gross was a prolific sijo poet. His sijo were witty, serious, or inspiring.

In the spring of 1996, Gross started *Sijo West: Journal of North American Sijo* as the editor, with Elizabeth St. Jacques as the associate editor. This quarterly journal drew international submissions of sijo as well as related articles, reviews, and art works. Due to illness of both editors, only five issues were published, spring 1998 being the last. Gross continued to run a couple of web sites dedicated to sijo. He created the *Sijo Forum* at Yahoo.com and was the moderator and teacher. Many aspiring sijo poets would post their sijo in this forum and receive feedback from Gross or other poets. When members posted questions, Gross answered each one with the utmost clarity and affection. Professor Gross passed away in 2014 and without his guidance the *Sijo Forum* became inactive. Gross wrote numerous articles on sijo writing. "The poet should not lose sight of three basic characteristics that make the sijo unique: its structure, its musical/rhythmic elements, and the twist which begins the final line. For best results, poets follow these guidelines very closely" (Gross).

He created a website, *Sijo Masters in Translation* (thewordshop.tripod.com/Sijo/masters.html) and posted sijo by Yun Son-do and seventeen other Korean sijo masters. He stated on the website:

> because of the drastic differences between languages, translators find literal translation of most Asian verses into English virtually impossible and unrewarding. Because of the nature of *hangul*, the official Korean script, that is more true of Korean verse than of most others. Translators, therefore, usually take one of two approaches: the meaning track or the poetic track. Translators who follow the meaning track attempt to stay as close as possible to literal meaning and structure. Too often the result can be choppy verse that obscures the energy and force of the original and does the original poet little justice.

Untitled

from *Sijo West #2,* Summer 1996

Rising early each morning,
I let her into the warm barn;
I pour oats, clean her stall,
then fork more hay into the trough;
When she kicks my hand away,
why do I think of my wife?

Untitled

from *Sijo Blossoms,* November 2001 (startag.tripod.com/Sijo.html)

Bark on the oak in the backyard
    has scars over my scars;
ladder steps lead nowhere now,
    swing rope has furrowed the old branch
How strong it makes us for a while —
    the world we make — before it goes.

Untitled

from *Sijo West* #2, Summer 1996

A welcome weekend at Cedar Key, relaxing on the dock;
pelicans wait poker-faced for bait fish we may leave behind.
Bob away, line, while I watch the sun going back to water.

ELIZABETH ST. JACQUES

Award-winning poet, Elizabeth St. Jacques, from Ontario, Canada, started learning haiku in the early 1970s. She stated in her book *Around the Tree of Light (Korean Sijo)* that she learned about Korean sijo from poetry contests. She self-studied sijo using Kim Unsong's book. She also stated that she was attracted to sijo because "sijo means literally songs for all seasons." She requested private advice from Kim Unsong and eventually won prizes from several sijo contests. Then she started contributing articles on *Sijo West* by Dr. Gross. She also started her own website [*SIJO In The Light (startag.tripod.com/SijoCont.html)*] in 1997.

St. Jacques posted an article on her website in 2001 titled "An Introduction to Sijo and Its Development in North America" where she stated that, "North American sijo in general differed from classical Korean sijo—in style, subject matter, expression, and line lengths. Indeed, sijo in North America was definitely being revolutionized. However, I was concerned: many poems didn't seem to be sijo at all." She went on to state that "while poets are free to make choices, they should not lose sight of three characteristics that make sijo unique: basic structure, musical/rhythmic elements, and the 'twist'". By 2001, sijo was included in poetry contests in Arizona, Florida, and North Carolina. St. Jacques won multiple prizes from these contests.

St. Jacques started communicating with Dr. Larry Gross of Florida and contributing articles on Dr. Gross' website. They both felt that preserving the sijo form was important and wrote guidelines for writing sijo in English. She stated that,

> The sijo is a three-line poem consisting of between forty-four to forty-six syllables. Each line has fourteen to fifteen syllables. Line one presents a problem or theme, line two develops or "turns" the thought, and line three resolves the problem or concludes the theme. The first half of the final line employs a "twist" by means of a surprise in meaning, sound, tone, or other device. To end with originality of wit, a profound observation or a strong emotional finale is a must. The sijo has a pleasing musical quality woven intricately throughout that is most important because even today, favorite sijo are sometimes sung or chanted. While imagery (metaphor, simile, pun, etc.) is employed in many sijo, it is not mandatory.

In the west, the sijo often appears as a six-line poem—that is, each of the three lines is broken in half, with each couplet separated by a blank line to emphasize distinctiveness. Presenting it this way facilitates printing (Gross).

Even Now
(in memory of St. Jacques' father)
from *Around the Tree of Light* by Elizabeth St. Jacques

Just us two in the photograph
    his arm around my thin shoulder

That strong limb I then leaned against
    would break so many falls

We stood like this but only once
    but his strength holds me still

For Love of Communication
from *Around the Tree of Light* by Elizabeth St. Jacques

Oh to know the languages
of all the peoples of the world

Harmonies await the ear
to solve all mysteries of tongues

Yet warm eyes open each closed door
smiles unfold blithe messages

White Water Path
from *Around the Tree of Light* by Elizabeth St. Jacques
Arizona State Poetry Society contest, first place winner 1993

Cruel river waters
    carried her true love away.
Roses weep from wilting branch
    and birdsongs echo requiems;
A floating trail of petals pale
    now softly lead the way to him.

LINDA SUE PARK

Linda Sue Park, an award-winning writer and poet, published her sijo collection *Tap Dancing On The Roof* in 2007. Park is the author of many books for young readers, including the 2002 Newbery Medal winner *A Single Shard* and the *New York Times* bestseller *A Long Walk to Water.*

During her early literary career, Park wrote novels set in ancient or medieval Korea. Park researched her Korean heritage for her books. Park stated that, while searching for Korean roots, she discovered sijo, and that led her to publish *Tap Dancing On The Roof.* Topics of her sijo include things children face in daily life at home or at school or in nature. For this picture book with poems, she won the Lion and the Unicorn Prize for Excellence in North American Poetry and ABC Children's Booksellers Choice Award.

Park wrote "some tips for writing your own sijo":

> Start with a single image or idea. Try to make the first line a complete unit of thought. This is easiest to do by writing it as one sentence. In the second line, develop the image further by adding details, description, or examples. Again, think of this line as a single unit or sentence. Advanced poets can try working with the stress count instead of with syllables. In this case, each line should have two halves, with three stresses in one half and four in the other (either 3/4 or 4/3). Most poets regard the last line—the "twist"—as the hardest part of writing sijo. I try to think of where the poem would go logically if I continued to develop the idea of the first two lines. Once I've figured that out, I write something that goes in the opposite direction—or at least "turns a corner" (Park).

School Lunch

from *Tap Dancing on the Roof* by Linda Sue Park

Each food plopped by tongs or spatula
into its own little space—
square pizza here, square brownie there;
milk carton cube, rectangle tray.

My snack at home after school?
Anything without corners.

Bedtime Snacks

from *Tap Dancing on the Roof* by Linda Sue Park

Good: Cookies and one glass of milk
for two dunkers—me and my dad.

Better: Popcorn, a video,
and sleeping bags stuffed with friends.

Best: Blanket pulled up over my head—
book, flashlight, and chocolate bar.

In 2021, Park published *The One Thing You'd Save*. When a teacher asks her class about the things they would save in an emergency, some students answer right away but others come to their decisions slowly. The book is written in three-line or linked verse, all inspired by the sijo form.

Untitled

from *The One Thing You'd Save* by Linda Sue Park

"C'mon, people—you hear me,
You gotta be real about this!
If a fire burns everything up,
You're gonna need money. *A lot.*
Am I the only one here with any smarts?
MY DAD'S WALLET. DUH."

MARK PETERSON

Mark Peterson received a doctorate in East Asian regional studies and East Asian languages and civilization from Harvard in 1987. As a faculty member of Brigham Young University since 1983, he coordinated the Asian Studies Program and taught Korean history and literature. After retirement, he established the non-profit research organization The Frog Outside the Well to change the direction of Korean history, establish understanding of Korean Confucianism, and foster the writing of sijo in Korean and English. He has published numerous articles and created his own YouTube channel teaching various topics on Korean history and culture including sijo. He has a passion for teaching English sijo to Americans. He wrote a few sijo himself. He is currently residing near Salt Lake City, Utah.

On Watching the Olympics

Nations of the world all gather
... in the little town of Sochi.
Athletes compete and cameras roll
... and the world's glued to TVs.
And for me, the experience revives memories
... of when the world came to Salt Lake.

ELIZABETH JORGENSEN

Elizabeth Jorgensen, author and sijo poet, is a high school English teacher who has been teaching not only students but other educators. As a prolific writer, she published her memoir, *Go, Gwen, Go: A Family's Journey to Olympic Gold*, and numerous articles on sijo-writing and teaching English sijo to high school students. She is a frequent speaker at state or national English teachers' conventions, including National Council of Teachers of English, Ohio Council of Teachers of English Language Arts, Wisconsin State Reading Association, and many others.

Untitled
Wisconsin Sijo Competition, runner-up 2021

I called on the smallest student, the one hiding in the back.

"I have nothing," she said. She cradled her head in her hands.
I didn't respond; instead, waited; willed her to fill the silence.

Senses

from *Gyroscope Review*, p. 44, Summer 2019.

He looks like crimson sunrises,
    smells like tangerine skies.
He tastes like silver shadows,
    sounds like Caribbean breezes.
But when he asks me to marry him,
    he feels like suffocation.

CHUCK NEWELL

Chuck Newell, an award-winning poet and educator, is the English department chair at Notre Dame High School in Chattanooga, Tennessee. He is a prolific writer of haiku and sijo.

Foggy Bridge

A lone ribbon of highway suspended above a still mountain lake.
Its beginning, its end obscured by morning fog, silent pines.
—a single car—arriving from nowhere, disappears into nothing.

Pandemic Time

Korean Cultural Center Los Angeles English Sijo Contest, third place 2020

In the east, the sun rises. It melts away the morning dew.
In the west, the sun sets. The last warmth of day fades over the hill.
This is how I mark pandemic time. The day, the month, matters not.

LUCY PARK

Lucy Park is one of the founding members and executive director of the Sejong Cultural Society, a non-profit based in Chicago. She's been teaching sijo to students and educators around the USA since 2008. Park wrote the following sijo in memory of her dear friend Sun who passed away recently.

In Memory of Sun

Just by looking at your big eyes,
    I used to start giggling.
Every time, when you spoke,
    I doubled up and rolled over laughing.
Since you left, I've not laughed.
    Are you making spirits laugh in heaven?

Sound of Winter

Freezing rain came all night,
    coating leaves and branches with thin ice.
When the bright morning sun shined,
    the tall tree sparkled like a huge gem.
Then heard the sound of winter;
    thousands of tiny gems falling to the ground.

OTHER SIJO POETS IN NORTH AMERICA

Other notable sijo poets in North America include Victor P. Gendrano (member of *Sijo Forum,* who published *Rustle of Bamboo Leaves: selected haiku and other poems,* 2005); Debra Woolard Bender (member of *Sijo Forum* who worked closely with Larry Gross and Elizabeth St. Jacques); Kirsty Karkow (member of *Sijo Forum,* published *Water Poems: Haiku, Tanka and Sijo,* 2005); R.W. Watkins (a Canadian poet who published

Wholly Trinities: The Nocturnal Iris Anthology of Sijo in English in 2020 and the editor of *Eastern Structures*, a journal dedicated to Asian poetry forms that includes sijo in every issue); Edward Baranosky (a poet and artist residing in Toronto, where he taught English sijo at poetry seminars); Tamara K. Walker (author and poet who published her sijo collection *Fabric Heart: A Collection of Contemporary Introspective Sijo* in 2019); Dina Cox (member of the *Sijo Forum*); and Yvonne Myers, among others. A majority of these poets are fluent in Japanese haiku, tanka, and other Asian poetry forms.

Bag Lady
by Victor P. Gendrano
from *Sijo Forum*

We called her the bag lady
    a fixture in the town square
She sat there with a toothless smile
    exchanging banters with the crowd
The bench is empty now, we learned
    a social worker picked her up

Untitled
by Kirsty Karkow
from *Water Poems*

in blue skies an osprey staggers,
    first a glide and then a stall
urgent peeps accompany the flaps,
    the falls, the twisting turns
on the nest, parents shriek with praise
    for a wild but fine first flight

Holiday Hangups

by Debra Woolard Bender

from *Wholly Trinities: The Nocturnal Iris Anthology of Sijo*

?
|
|
0
^

to make ready
for the holidays,
I've traveled 'round my house;

dustrag and broom, mop and vacuum,
all the rooms are polished clean.

limp and dirty, I could pass
as an old
cleaning
rag!

?
|
|
0
^

miracle,
you must be here...
do you wonder when I'll notice?

hustle and bustle wrap the world,
disguised as Christmas spirit.

come and find me, miracle!
ollie ollie oxen
free!

?
|
|
0
^

noise, oh noise,
please won't you stop?
house full, I long for silence;

a wave, a kiss, away they go
with tinseled trees & colored lights.

even the winter garden's
emptier than before

Works Cited

Azalea: Journal of Korean Literature and Culture. University of Hawaii Press, 2011.

This work appears with permission of the Harvard University Korea Institute from David R. McCann, *Azalea: A Journal of Korean Literature and Culture* Volume 4 (Cambridge, Mass: Harvard University Korea Institute, 2011), © The President and Fellows of Harvard College, 2011.

Cho, Oh-hyun. *For Nirvana: 108 Zen Sijo Poems.* New York, Columbia University Press, 2016.

Gendrano, Victor P. *Rustle of Bamboo Leaves: Selected Haiku and Other Poems.* Morrisville, North Carolina, Lulu Enterprises, Inc., 2005.

Gross, Larry. *Asian Poetry: The Korean Sijo*
https://bit.ly/3iut5TK

Gross, Larry. *Sijo Masters in Translation*
https://bit.ly/2U2swXZ

Gross, Larry and Elizabeth St. Jacques. *Sijo West, Journal of North American Sijo.* Vol.1-2, Tallahassee Florida, 1996-1998.

Gyroscope Review, Summer, 2019.

Im, Jong-chan. *Potato Flower,* Sejong Publisher, 2017.

Karkow, Kirsty. *Water Poems.* Black Cat Press, Eldersburg, Maryland, 2005.

Kim, Jaihiun. *Modern Korean Verse in Sijo Form.* Vancouver, BC, Ronsdale Press, 1997.

Kim, Unsong. *100 Classical Korean Poems (Sijo).* Selected and translated by Kim Unsong, POET Vol.27, No.3., 1986.

Kim, Unsong. *Poems of Modern Sijo.* California, One Mind Press, 1995.

McCann, David R. *Urban Temple. Sijo, Twisted and Straight.* Bo-Leaf

Books, 2008.

Park, Linda Sue. *Tap Dancing On the Roof.* New York, Houghton Mifflin Harcourt, 2007.

Park, Linda Sue. *The One Thing You'd Save.* Clarion Books, 2021.

Rutt, Richard. *The Bamboo Grove: An Introduction to Sijo.* University of Michigan Press, 1998.

St. Jacques, Elizabeth. *Around the Tree of Light.* Ontario, Canada, Maplebud Press, 1995.

St. Jacques, Elizabeth. *In the Light: Sijo.*
https://bit.ly/386Gzio

Seo, Kwan-ho. *Sijo Even My Puppies Know (강아지도 아는 시조).* Children's Sijo World Publisher, 2017.

Sijo Blossoms, November 2001
https://bit.ly/3zbF3HI

Watkins, R.W. Ed. *Wholly Trinities. The Nocturnal Iris Anthology of Sijo in English.* Nocturnal Iris Publications, 2020.

Sijo Written in Other Languages

Lucy Park

Sijo can be written in languages other than Korean or English. Here are sijo written in German, Tagalog, Russian, Spanish, and Swahili.

SIJO IN GERMAN

Chon Young-Ae, professor emeritus of German literature at Seoul National University, in the chapter "IM LIED JEDOCH – in der globalisierten Welt. Korea-Gedichte von Reiner Kunze" of her book *Grenzgänge der poetischen Sprache* (2013), described sijo written by esteemed German poet Reiner Kunze. Kunze's poetry book *lindennacht* (2007) contains twelve poems with striking lyrical images of Korea's past and present, including a sijo. Below is an excerpt from Professor Chon's book.

Koreanische Legende in Altem Stil

Dem könig, dem er treue schwor, die treue haltend, schied
der weise vom verschwörer. Seines mörders blick er mied
rücklings auf die Brücke reitend ins gezückte schwert, ins lied.

    Kunze wrote this poem after reading a sijo exchange between Jeong Mong-ju (1337-1392) and Yi Bang-won (1367-1422). The occasion was the takeover of power in 1392, in which the Goryeo dynasty (918-1392) was replaced by the Joseon dynasty (1392-1910). It is about the dialogue that Jeong Mong-ju, a loyal subject of the Goryeo dynasty, and the son of the usurper Yi Bang-won conducted shortly before the change of power. Yi Bang-won invited Jeong to a drink in a pavilion and asked an apparently naïve, harmless question in the form of a sijo:

이런 들 어떠하리 저런들 어떠하리
만수산 두렁칡이 얽혀진들 어떠하리
우리도 이같이 얽혀 한 백년 살아보세

Was macht dies aus, was macht das aus, lass es so.
Auf dem Mansu-Berg wächst das wilde Geranke zusammen, lass es so.
Auch wir können so zusammen hundert Jahre genießen.

What difference does it make,
    this way or that?
The tangled vines of Mansu San
    in profusion grow entwined.
We too could be like that,
    and live together a hundred years.

        German translation by Chon Young-Ae
        English translation by Inez Kong Pai

The answer of the loyal subject looks equally apolitical:

이몸이 죽고죽어 일 백번 고쳐죽어
백골이 진토되어 넋이라도 있고없고
님 향한 일편 단심이야 가실줄이 있으랴

Mein Köper kann sterben und sterben, hundertmal wieder sterben.
Meine weißen Gebeine zerfallen zu Staub, zu Lehm, mit oder ohne Seele.
Meine Treue dem Geliebten gegenüber würde um keinen Deut verblassen.

Though I die, and die again,
　　Though I die one hundred deaths,
After my bones have turned to dust,
　　Whether my soul exists or not,
My red heart, forever loyal to my Lord,
　　Will never fade away.

　　　German translation by Chon Young-Ae
　　　English translation by Mark Peterson

Behind this poetic-political dialogue the insight into the seriousness of the situation as well as into a difficult decision that has now been made becomes recognizable. After this conversation, which was polite and harmonious, the loyal subject left the pavilion, rode home, but was already sitting backwards on the horse so as not to have to look his murderers in the face. And in fact he was slain on a bridge (선죽교, Seonjuk-gyo) on the way. This primal scene has retrospectively shaped this form of poetry in its creation phase. The sijo was almost the only genus that was cultivated throughout the five hundred years of the Joseon dynasty.

Reiner Kunze takes on this historical material in one of his Korea poems in *lindennacht* and gives it—not only in terms of content, but also form-determining—an impressive outline:

Koreanische Legende in Altem Stil

Dem könig, dem er treue schwor, die treue haltend, schied
der weise vom verschwörer. Seines mörders blick er mied
rücklings auf die Brücke reitend ins gezückte schwert, ins lied.

XXX XXXXX XXX XXX
XXX XXXX XXXX XXX
XXX XXXXX XXXX XXX
(syllable counts in German)

A Korean Legend in Old Korean Style

Faithful to his king to whom he swore allegiance, the wise man
Left the usurper. He avoided the gaze of his murderer
Riding backwards onto the bridge; into the drawn sword, into the song.

The poetic transformation has already been strikingly successful in terms of form: In a form that is just as compressed as in the original, the content is first reproduced true to the number of syllables (14, 14, 15), with the slightly varying last line, according to the original scheme, exhibiting an expansion small in form but significant in content. Even the internal units within a line are implemented—in the first with a comma and in the second with a point. The formal parallelism that characterizes the first and second lines in the original scheme (3 4 3 4 | 3 4 3 4) is reflected in the varying and increasing repetitions—in the first line with "loyal swore" and "loyal keeping", in the second line "(the wise man) left the usurper. He avoided the gaze of his murderer; they underline the importance of the content.

The end rhyme is also realized even more artfully than in the original. The weight of the whole thing is concentrated on the three monosyllabic rhyming words, which firmly connect three verses as a unit and at the same time contain a moment of improvement: "schied/left"— "mied/avoided"—"lied/song". In terms of content, they are the decisive bearers of importance. The end rhyme—which is not necessary in the original scheme—emphasizes here, in these three lines, not only a story in poetic form and with personal imprint, but also the transformation of a story into poetry: The ride of a faithful "into the drawn sword" here at the same time represents the ride "into the song". As a result, the lasting effects of that politically upright posture, but also the poeticization itself and its process, are made clear in the poem. In this regard, Reiner Kunze realizes in his poem what the two poems mean today in retrospect; the two men Jeong and Yi themselves could not yet be aware of the formative effect of their poems. Here is a decisive further development: in no way an antiquated, imitative experiment, but a remarkable innovation.

What this one short poem—over six hundred years ago—transferred to the other end of the world is a valuable cultural asset. In the volume of poetry *lindennacht* there are eleven other poems that touch on this topic. Each is a highly poetic achievement that points to a different possibility of access to the foreign: beyond all possible—missionary, colonial, globalized capitalist, tourist—interest speaks from this real sympathy (Chon 151-168).

Chon, Young-Ae is Professor Emerita of German Literature at Seoul National University and a poet. She was the president of the Korean Goethe Society, a senior fellow at the Freiburg Institute for Advanced Studies, and is currently a member of the Research Center of the Klassik Stiftung Weimar. Her monographs include *"Wie sprech'auch ich so schön?"*, *"Zur Macht der Poesie bei Goethe* (Wallstein, 2011)", *"Sich erbittend ew'es Leben"*, and *"Sieben Essays zu Goethes West-östlichen Divan"* (Wallenstein, 2017). She also published her translations of the works of Goethe, Rilke, Kafka, Celan, Christa Wolf, Reiner Kunze and many other German writers and poets into Korean. As a poet, she published seven poetry books in both Korean and German. Chon is a recipient of numerous awards including Die Goldene Goethe—

Medaille (The Golden Goethe—Medal of Goethe Society in Weimar, 2011), The Prize for the Best Teaching of Seoul National University (2011), The Samsung—Prize for Creative Women (2020), Mirok-Li Prize of the German-Korean Society and the Korean-German Society (2021) and Reiner Kunze Prize (2021).

Reiner Kunze (born 16 August 1933 in Oelsnitz, Erzgebirge, Saxony) is a German writer and GDR (German Democratic Republic; East Germany) dissident. He studied media and journalism at the University of Leipzig. In 1968, he left the GDR state party SED (Socialist Unity Party of East Germany) following the communist Warsaw Pact countries invasion of Czechoslovakia in response to the Prague Spring. His books had to be published in West Germany since his book was forbidden from publication in East Germany, which made him leave his homeland. In 1976, his most famous book *The Lovely Years*, which contained critical insights into life, and the policies behind the Iron Curtain, was published in West Germany to great acclaim. In 1977, the GDR regime expatriated him, and he moved to West Germany (FRG). He now lives near Passau in Bavaria. His writings consist mostly of poetry, though he wrote prose as well, including essays: *Sensible Wege* (1969), *Deckname Lyrik* (1990). *lindennacht* (2007), *die stunde mit dir selbst* (2018). He is also a translator of Czech poetry and prose. Kunze was a victim of the Stasi's Zersetzung psychological warfare program. He was awarded many prizes including Georg Trakl-Preis, Georg Büchner Prize, Friedrich-Hölderlin-Preis, the Thüringer Literaturpreis and many more.

Sijo in Tagalog

by Victor P. Gendrano

from *Rustle of Bamboo Leaves: Selected haiku and other poems*

Anahaw Palm

nang ikaw ay makakita
ng damit na payong

iniwanan mong kusa
ang anahaw na pandong

ngunit nang mapunit
bumalik ka rin sa dahon

(English version)
Anahaw Palm

when you found an umbrella
to shade you from the sun and rain

you discarded the anahaw leaf
you used and grew up with

but when the wind ripped its cloth
to the lowly frond you returned

Homeland

ang halik ng bumaba't tumaas na alon
sa malayong pampang

mainit na hangin at ulan

sa luntiang lupa'y nagbibigay huhay

mga tao'y maka-Diyos at pangkaraniwan
iyan ang aking bayan

(English Version)
Homeland

the ebb and flow of rolling waves
caress the isle's distant shore

where balmy breeze and tropical rains
nourish the verdant plains

peopled by God-fearing simple folks
the place I call my home

American poet Victor P. Gendrano (1959-2018) described himself as "not beholden to a particular time or place with its physical boundaries" in his book of poems *Rustle of Bamboo Leaves: Selected haiku and other poems*. Gendrano was a prolific writer of haiku, tanka, sijo, American cinquain, and free verse in English and Tagalog. He was an active member of Sijo Forum, World Haiku Club, and Haiku Society of America. His poems were published in *World Haiku Review, Lynx: Journal for Linking Poets, Stylus Poetry Journal, Simply Haiku, The Heron's Nest, Amaze: Cinquain Journal, Hijinx*, and many other magazines. Gendrano was born and raised in the Philippines, earned a bachelor's degree from the University of Philippines at Los Baños, and graduated with a master's degree from Syracuse University in New York.

Sijo in Russian

by Sasha A. Palmer

На окне в простой склянке свежая ветвь азалии
макает нежный бутон в прозрачную голубизну.
Художник! Сломай свою кисть, брось рисовать — лишь смотри.

This Russian sijo follows the traditional syllabic structure (3-4-4-4; 3-4-4-4; 3-5-4-3) with the third line split into the counter-theme and conclusion:

На окне (3 syllables)| в простой склянке (4)| свежая ветвь (4)| азал ии (4)

макает (3)| нежный бутон (4)| в прозрачную (4)| голубизну. (4)

Художник! (3)| Сломай свою кисть, (5)|| брось рисовать — (4)| ли шь смотри. (3)

(English version)
On the sill in a plain glass a freshly cut azalea
is dipping a tender bud in the blueness of clear water.
O artist! Destroy your brushes, no more painting—simply look.

Sasha A. Palmer is a Russian-born award-winning poet and translator, who currently lives in Baltimore, Maryland. Palmer's work appeared in *Writer's Digest, Slovo/Word, Cardinal Points,* and elsewhere. She tries to follow the motto she has created: Live for the Love of it. Visit Sasha at www.sashaapalmer.com

Sijo in Spanish

by Dana Patterson Nelson

Controlar

Cada noche me escapo a un mundo diferente
Desde mi cama, uno toque controla mi realidad
El tele pierde su agarre cuando llega el sueño.

4-4-4-4
5-4-3-4
3-6-4-3

(English Version)
Control

Every night I escape to inviting worlds to avoid sleep
Reclined in bed, eyelids shutter; mindless touches control reality
Mounted screen loosens its grip; as I yield to needed slumber

Dana Patterson Nelson is Secondary English Instruction Special Education Coordinator and Assistant Director of Special Education at the Kansas Public Schools in Kansas City, Missouri. She earned two masters degrees in Special Education and Education Administration, and is currently working on her Masters in Divinity. While she lived in Qatar in the Middle East, she trained Qatari educators. She worked extensively with groups in Ghana and Colombia. She is a member of the Kansas Governor's Council on Education. She is fluent in multiple languages. After learning English sijo, she has been experimenting with Spanish, Swahili, Pidgin, Creole, and Patois.

Nelson stated, "I found the process of writing first in Spanish for sijo to be interesting. Spanish is laden with syllables and because it has masculine/feminine nouns with accompanying articles (i.e., el/la, un/uno/una, los/las, unos/unas). So it uses more syllables than its English translation. I wrote mine first in Spanish then adapted/translated it into English. Had I done the inverse, the Spanish wouldn't have conformed at all to sijo syllabic structure."

Sijo in Swahili

by Dana Patterson Nelson

Amani inasubiri kwa utulivu kwangu
Nasubiri sauti yake, mwongozo na rafiki
Kama sisikii chochote, machafuko yanarudi.
3-5-5-2
4-5-3-4
5-3-4-4

(English version)
Peace awaits patiently and still freely choosing me alone
I wait without worry for her silken voice, a guide and friend
If I hear nothing but eerie quiet; disrupting chaos returns.

Works Cited

Chon, Young-Ae. *Im Lied Jedoch-in globalisierten Welt. Korea-Gedichte von Reiner Kunze.*

Chon, Young-Ae: *Grenzgänge der poetischen Sprache.* Würzburg, 2013.

Gendrano, Victor P. *Rustle of Bamboo Leaves: Selected haiku and other poems.* Lulu Enterprises, 2005.

Sijo and Music

Lucy Park

1. *Sijo Chang* (시조창) in Ancient Korea

In ancient Korea, sijo poets sang sijo. It is only recently, in the early twentieth century, that sijo poets started writing sijo for reading or reciting. Sijo singing is known as *sijo chang* (시조창) in Korea and is recognized as a genre of traditional Korean music. Sijo poems are written in three lines: *cho-jang* (초장 first-line), *joong-jang* (중장 second line), and *jong-jang* (종장 third line). The sijo poems are sung in three-, four- or five-note melodic scales and are typically sung in a deliberate, very slow tempo using a fixed rhythmic pattern. A *sijo chang* performance includes a vocalist and a percussion accompaniment on the *jang-gu*. The *jang-gu* is an hourglass-shaped drum and the most widely used percussion instrument in Korean music or dance performance. Sometimes singers are joined by wind instruments made of bamboo, such as *daegum, danso,* or *piri*.

During the Joseon dynasty (1392-1910), the center of musical activities moved from the royals to commoners. The musical scene included the middle class, who accumulated significant wealth, the upper class who were pushed out of political main stages, and intellectuals who were critical of the ruling class. Among all types of music, vocal music including *sijo chang* was the most popular genre.

Sijo chang was frequently sung by professionals. At private gatherings, poets sang their own sijo at impromptu performances. Descriptions of *sijo chang* appear in books written in the seventeenth century including *Paik-eun-am Gum-bo* (백운암금보) by Eo-eun-bo (어은보); and in the eighteenth century, *Seok-book-gyb* (석북집) by Shin Gwang-soo.

Sijo chang was sung in different melodic scales. The most common and basic type is *Pyung sijo* (평시조). The *Pyung sijo* (평시조), sung in regions close to Seoul, is called *Kyung-je* (경제) and uses a three-note melodic scale. The sijo originated from the Seoul region; therefore, *Kyung-je* was the genesis of *sijo chang*. The *sijo chang* in other regions are known as *Hyang-je* (향제) and include *Young-je* (영제) from *Gyung-sang* region (경상도 지역), *Wan-je* (완제) from *Jun-ra* region (전라도 지역), *Naepo-je* (내포제) from *Choong-chung* region (충청도지역), and others.

Sijo chang includes stylistic variations known as *Joong-heo-ri sijo* (중허리시조), *Ji-rum sijo* (지름시조), *Sa-seol ji-rum sijo* (사설지름시조), and *Soo-jap-ga sijo* (수잡가). The *Pyung sijo* (평시조) starts songs in middle range; *Joong-heo-ri sijo* (중허리시조) uses high notes on the third beat of the first line (초장); *Ji-rum sijo* (지름시조) also typically starts songs with a high note (Kim, Hae-sook et al. 178-180).

2. KOREAN ART SONGS WITH SIJO

Korean art songs are popular among Koreans and are composed in the western music tradition. Some earlier songs are written in a style similar to German *lied* or French *mélodie* but with distinct Korean emotion. Korean art songs started to appear in the early twentieth century. Composers such as Hong Nan-pa

(홍난파 1897-1941) and Hyun Je-myung (현제명 1902-1960) were pioneers of Korean art songs in the 1920s. They learned western music from Christian missionaries and went to the United States for further study. Their songs were simple, sorrowful, and sometimes included an element of folk songs. After Korea gained liberation from Japanese rule, many composers wrote songs with high-level artistry and produced new kinds of Korean art songs. During the Korean war, many Korean art songs expressed the hardships of the nation. After the war, the popularity of Korean art songs continued to grow and new pieces included songs with humor and patriotic themes.

Several years ago, I came across the Korean art song "Stars" (별). This is one of my favorite Korean art songs. I realized the lyrics of this song are a sijo written by Yi Pyong-gi (이병기) who is a well-known sijo poet and one of the pioneers of modern sijo. Since the structure of sijo has musical beats (with syllable counts of 3-4-4-4, 3-4-4-4, 3-5-4-3), it can be made into songs quite easily. I searched out other Korean art songs and found several more with sijo. Most of these songs are beloved by Koreans: "Spring Maiden" (봄처녀, lyrics by Yi Un-sang and music by Hong Nan-pa), "The Swing" (그네, lyrics by Kim Mal-bong and music by Gum Su-hyun), and "Nostalgia" (가고파, by Yi Un-sang and music by Kim Dong-jin).

Video recordings of the following art songs from the Poetry Foundation and the International Music Foundation are on the Sejong Cultural Society YouTube channel: "Nostalgia" (가고파), "Spring Maiden" (봄처녀), and "The Swing" (그네).

3. Contemporary Classical Music and Jazz Inspired by Sijo

In 2017, I met Stephen Young, program director of the Poetry Foundation, to plan a concert, "Poetry and Music", at the foundation's beautiful lecture hall. I wanted to include a broad spectrum of musical genres in order to reach people with different musical tastes. I decided to include classical, contemporary classical, jazz, and hip-hop. Three composers, Ted Niedermaier (Roosevelt University, classical), Misook Kim (Wheaton Conservatory, classical), and Scott Hall (Columbia College, jazz) were invited to compose a piece with sijo. The final program was titled "Music Inspired by Korean Poetry: Sijo Poems in Settings from Classical to Hip-Hop". Video recordings of this concert are on the Sejong Cultural Society YouTube Channel.

In 2019, we presented another concert "Sijo Poetry" at the Rush Hour Concerts at St. James Cathedral in downtown Chicago. This renowned concert series is well-known to Chicago classical music lovers as they present the best of Chicago-based classical artists in chamber music recitals. Video recording of this concert can be found on the Sejong Cultural Society YouTube Channel.

4. Sijo-Inspired Hip-Hop

I wanted to create youth appeal by bridging the gap between traditional sijo and contemporary pop music. I began to work with Elephant Rebellion (ER), a Chicago-based community-oriented artists' collective, and selected hip-hop as our medium. ER uses sijo as inspiration for their hip-hop lyrics. They use a variety of sijo, from traditional classic poems, to a winner's sijo from the Sejong Writing Competition, and even poems the members themselves write. As a group of musicians with diverse ethnic backgrounds, many of them first-generation immigrants and minorities, ER jumped at the chance to use twelfth-grade student Roberto Santos' 2013 first-place sijo.

Still American

They say go, return to land that I don't know. It makes no sense.
Born and raised American, so Mexico is still foreign.
Culture kept, but this is my home. Immigrant, no: Hispanic.

Since sijo is only three lines, they used Santos' sijo as the refrain and each ER member wrote a sijo to go with the refrain. Full text of this hip-hop song is at the end of this chapter.

5. FUTURE DIRECTION OF SIJO AND MUSIC

The sijo, by nature, is ideal for making songs as one can sing the sijo in any musical genre. Some may say it would be easy to make sijo songs because you can write sijo in multiple stanzas. Such sijo are known as "chain of sijo" or "sijo sequence (연시 조)". Or as ER demonstrated, one sijo can be used as a refrain and multiple verses can be added between refrains. A poet can write an entire sijo in this way. Or several people may write together; each person writes one verse and then a refrain is written jointly. Another approach is writing linked sijo. Linked sijo can be written by one poet or several poets. Elizabeth St. Jacques, a Canadian sijo poet, explained how it works.

> Poet #1 writes a sijo to which the second poet's sijo links in some way to the first. Poet #1 writes another sijo that links to the second poem, and so on. To link, choose an image, color, sound, sensation, sentiment, or whatever from the newest sijo and respond with a link that is not too obvious.

Each link connects only with the preceding sijo, never with earlier or later sijo. It is important that each sijo stands by itself and each link shifts in a new direction. This takes us on a fascinating and surprising journey that makes linked poetry unique and challenging (St. Jacques).

In sijo sequence, each sijo focuses on one overall theme. A sequence may consist of any number of sijo. Most modern Korean sijo poets write "chain of sijo" or "sijo sequence (연시조)" as you can see in the following examples of Korean art songs.

KOREAN ART SONGS WITH SIJO

Spring Maiden
봄 처녀
sijo by Yi Un-sang, music by Hong Nan-pa (이은상 시, 홍난파 곡)
translation by Kim Jaihiun, from *Modern Korean Verse in Sijo Form*

Here comes at last our Spring Maid
    dressed in shoots of grass,
veiled in a fleecy cloud,
    shod with pearls of dew.
Who will she be meeting,
    a bouquet pinned on her breast?

Will she ever pass my house
    on her way to meet her lover?
Or is she coming for me?
    I don't know.
Shall I go and make a fool of myself
    and ask her where she is going?

봄 처녀 제 오시네. 새 풀옷을 입으셨네
하얀 구름 너울 쓰고 진주이슬 신으셨네
꽃다발 가슴에 안고 뉘를 찾아 오시는고

님 찾아 가는 길에 내 집 앞을 지나시나
이상도 하오시라 행여 내게 오심인가
미안코 어리석은 양 나가 물어 볼까나

Love
사랑
sijo by Yi Un-sang, music by Hong Nan-pa (이은상 시, 홍난파 곡)
translation by Jean Kim and Lucy Park

If you're going to burn, burn it all, don't only burn halfway
Burn and burn, again and again, turn it all to ash
If it's only half-burned, it's no good

Don't even start to burn if you'll only go halfway
If you'll only make an attempt, just forget about it
If you are going to burn, burn up even the ashes

탈대로 다 타시오 타다 말진 부디마소
타고 다시 타서 재될법은 하거니와
타다가 남은 동강은 쓰을 곳이 없느니다

반타고 꺼질진대 애제 타지 말으시오
차라리 아니타고 생낙으로 잊으시오
탈진댄 재 그것조차 마저 탐이 옳으니다

The　Swing
그네
sijo by Kim Mal-Bong, music by Gum Su-Hyon (김말봉 시, 금수현 곡)
translation by Gyung-ryul Jang

Jade-colored fine ramie-cloth skirt and gilt pigtail ribbon
Are leaping into the blue sky and fluttering in the clouds.
A startled swallow stares at them, forgetting to beat its wings.

As she pushes off once, she soars as high as to the treetop.
As she pushes off twice, the world lays itself flat beneath her feet.
Myriad worries of the mind are all blown away in the wind.

세모시 옥색치마 금박 물린 저 댕기가
창공을 차고 나가 구름 속에 나부낀다
제비도 놀란 양 나래 쉬고 보더라

한 번 구르니 나무 끝에 아련하고
두 번을 거듭 차니 사바가 발 아래라
마음의 일만 근심은 바람이 실어가네

Stars
별
sijo by Yi Pyong-gi, music by Lee Soo-In (이병기 시, 이수인 곡)
translation by Kim Jaihiun, from *Modern Korean Verse in Sijo Form*

The air is cool and pleasant as I step into my courtyard.
The sky has cleared above the peaks to the west.
And a slice of moon appears with the coming of the stars.

Now the moon sinks, the stars signal to one another.
Whose stars can they be? Which one is mine?
Standing alone in the night, I count them one by one.

바람이 서늘도 하여 뜰 앞에 나섰더니
서산머리에 하늘은 구름을 벗어나고
산뜻한 초사흘달이 별과 함께 나오더라

달은 넘어 가고 별만 서로 반짝인다
저 별은 뉘 별이며 내 별 또 어느 게요

잠자코 호올로 서서 별을 헤어 보노라

Nostalgia
가고파

sijo by Yi Un-sang, music by Kim Dong-jin (이은상 시, 김동진 곡)

translation by Gyung-ryul Jang

Vividly I see in my mind's eye the Southern Sea so blue and serene.
How can I forget even in dreams the serene waters of my hometown?
Even now, the seabirds would greet me. Oh, I wish I were back home!

I miss those friends of mine whom I played with when I was a child.
Wherever I go and wherever I am, how can I ever forget them?
How are they doing these days? Oh, I wish I met them again!

While seabirds and friends are all still there at my hometown,
How and why have I come to leave my hometown and live alone?
Shall I go back home right now, leaving everything behind?

Oh, how I long to go back home and mingle with them as before!
How I long to live there and laugh as I did as a child in festive attire!
How I long to go back to those days when there were no tears at all!

내 고향 남쪽 바다 그 파란물 눈에 보이네
꿈엔들 잊으리요 그 잔잔한 고향바다
지금도 그 물새들 날으리 가고파라 가고파

어릴 제 같이 놀던 그 동무들 그리워라
어디 간들 잊으리요 그 뛰놀던 고향 동무
오늘은 다 무얼 하는고 가고파라 가고파

그 물새 그 동무들 고향에 다 있는데
나는 왜 어이타가 떠나 살게 되었는고
온갖 것 다 뿌리치고 돌아갈까 돌아가

가서 한데 얼려 옛날같이 살고 지고
내 마음 색동옷 입혀 웃고 웃고 지내고저
그날 그 눈물 없던 때를 찾아가자 찾아가

> **Editor's note:** This sijo is written in ten verses. Kim Dong-jin composed a song using the first four verses in 1932-1933. In 1973, Kim composed songs for the last six verses. The first four-verse song is the most popular among all Korean art songs and performed frequently even in present day.

CLASSICAL MUSIC INSPIRED BY SIJO

Trio by Teddy Niedermaier
inspired by sijo by Yi Myonghan, Hwang Chini, and Yang Sa-on

Untitled
by Yi Myonghan (1595-1645)
translation by Richard Rutt, from *Bamboo Grove: An Introduction to Sijo*

If on the pathways of dreams
    a footprint could leave a mark
The road by your window
    though rough with rocks,
would soon wear smooth.
    But in dreams paths take no footprints.
I mourn the more for that.

꿈에 다니는 길이 자최곳 나랑이면
님의 집 窓(창) 밖의 石路(석로)라도 달으련마는
꿈길이 자최 업스니 그를 슬허하노라

Untitled
by Hwang Chini (probably 1506-1567)

translation by David McCann, from *Early Korean Literature: Selections and Introductions*

Jade Green Stream, don't boast so proud
    of your easy passing through these blue hills.
Once you have reached the broad sea,
    to return again will be hard.
While the Bright Moon fills these empty hills,
    why not pause? Then go on, if you will.

청산리 청산리 벽계수야 수이감을 자랑마라
일도 창해하면 다시오기 어려오니
명월이 만강산하니 쉬여간들 엇더리

Untitled
by Yang Sa-on(1517-1584)
translation by Kevin O'Rourke, from *The Sijo Tradition*

The mountain may be high,
    But it is still below heaven
Climb and climb again;
    Everyone can reach the summit
Only the man who never tried
    insists the mountain is high.

태산이 높다하되 하늘아래 뫼이로다
오르고 또 오르면 못오를리 없건만은
사람이 제 아니 오르고 뫼만 높다 하더라

JAZZ ENSEMBLE INSPIRED BY SIJO

by Scott Hall, inspired by "Tennis" by Linda Sue Park

Tennis
by Linda Sue Park
from *Tap Dancing on the Roof*

When the professionals play,
it's like watching a metronome:
Racquet to racquet and back again,
the ball keeps a perfect, steady beat.
When I'm on the court with my friends,
we improvise: jazz, hip-hop.

SIJO-INSPIRED HIP-HOP SONG

They Say Go
by Elephant Rebellion
hip-hop song based on **Still American** by Roberto Santos

> ***Editor's note:*** Although Santos wrote "Hispanic" at the end of his sijo, ER changed the word to "Latino" in their song, because it is easier to sing. Elephant Rebellion wrote two more songs titled "Sijo Seas" and "Be Here" using sijo for the refrains.

refrain **Still American** by Roberto Santos

They say go, return to land that I don't know. It makes no sense.
Born and raised American, so Mexico is still foreign.
Culture kept, but this is my home. Immigrant, no: Latino!

verse by Ona Wong

Learn English: the official language. This is America.
Are you dumb? That's what they say:
Teachers, couns'lers, special ed class.
Speaking Shawnee on First Nations Land.
America. Where is that?

verse **Fu Gee La** by Uran Kabashi

It's hard for me, to speak the past, a refugee, a lethal path
But now I'm here, awoken life, it's broken right, there's hope tonight
open lights, and then I speak the truth, at an open mic, with the youth

verse by Mewael 'MO Beats' Michael

I hear a sound that is shockingly disturbing my sweet dreams
They call it an alarm clock, and it's supposed to wake you up
But when I wake up, I feel more asleep than when I'm dreaming

verse by Lorena Buñi

She left home borrowed money took a plane to a foreign land.
She worked hard for her young child, her aging mom and ailing dad.
Now she's home, in the balikbayan box she is flown in, modern day slave.

verse by Mergen Batdelger

I say, I cannot for I have never attempted
I don't know for I have yet to unravel the truth
But how dare I answer questions I have yet to question
always been a foreigner on a quest,
alienated based on where I was born at

verse by Angel Pantoja

They call my people criminals
saying we've stolen all their jobs
We who leave behind our dynasties
to work in fields all day
America you criminals;
let us correct your twisted ways

verse by Micah Gray

Who can stop humanity's
Deceptive ways can someone see
It is me the one who lives
Searching for love in this new age
Gifted be the messenger who flies ahead with (battered wings)

Works Cited

Kim, Haesook, Paik Dae-woong, Choi Tai-hyun. *Introduction to Traditional Korean Music* (전통음악개론). Eu-ul-rim (어울림) Publisher, 1995.

Kim, Jaihiun. *Modern Korean Verse in Sijo Form.* Vancouver, BC, Ronsdale Press, 1997.

McCann, David R. *Early Korean Literature: Selections and Introductions.* New York, Columbia Press, 2000.

Music inspired by Korean Poetry: Sijo poems in Settings from Classical to Hip-hop. (2017 at the Poetry Foundation, Chicago) Concert program. https://bit.ly/3AkJW1p

Video recording of above concert. https://bit.ly/3lJ9dhQ

Sijo Poetry. Rush Hour Concerts. in collaboration with the Poetry Foundation and the Sejong Cultural Society. (2019 at the St. James Cathedral, Chicago) Concert program. https://bit.ly/3mhTaYl

Video recording of the Rush Hour Concert. https://bit.ly/3z4CCqy

O'Rourke, Kevin. *The Sijo Tradition*. Seoul, Korea, Jung Eum Sa, Seoul, 1987.

Park, Linda Sue. *Tap Dancing on the Roof*. Houghton Mifflin Harcourt Publishing, 2007.

Rutt, Richard. *The Bamboo Grove: An Introduction to Sijo*. University of Michigan Press, 1998.

St Jacques, Elizabeth. *How To Write Linked Sijo and Sijo Sequences*. 1996, revised March 2001. https://bit.ly/2WalKAy

Cultural Dimension in Sijo Translation and Variations of Sijo Format

Seong-Kon Kim

1. Cultural Translation of Sijo

Since the Tower of Babel, humans have needed interpreters and translators to communicate across nations. Due to cultural differences, however, misunderstandings often arise, and sometimes things are inevitably lost in translation. That is why there is a saying that "every translator is a traitor."

A host of writers have contemplated and written about the innate problems of translation. For example, Yevgeny Yevtushenko humorously wrote, "Translation is like a woman. If it is beautiful, it is not faithful. If it is faithful, it is most certainly not beautiful." If he had said it today, he could not have avoided harsh criticism from feminists. Nevertheless, Yevtushenko tried to point out an inherent problem of translation.

Robert Frost, too, pointed out the problem of poetry translation: "Poetry is what gets lost in translation." Samuel Johnson joined Frost by arguing, "Poetry cannot be translated. But as the beauties of poetry cannot be preserved in any language except that in which it was originally written, we learn the language." According to Johnson, we should read poetry in its original language, not in translation. The problem is that not many are willing to learn a new language to read poetry.

George Borrow has disparaged translation, saying, "Translation is at best an echo." Virginia Woolf also lamented the difficulty of rendering humor in a foreign language: "Humor is the first of the gifts to perish in a foreign language." Indeed, translating humor into another language is extremely difficult and tricky because sense of humor varies from one culture to another.

At the same time, however, other intellectuals have acknowledged the importance of translation. For example, Jose Saramago once wrote, "Writers make national literature, while translators make universal literature." As Paul Auster put it, "Translators are the shadow heroes of literature, the often forgotten instruments that make it possible for different cultures to talk to one another, who have enabled us to understand that we all, from every part of the world, live in one world." Anthony Burgess, too, once said, "Translation is not a matter of words only; it is a matter of making intelligible a whole culture."

Simply reading a translation and fully understanding the cultural milieu of a literary work are two different things. Sometimes foreigners may interpret a faithfully translated literary text differently. When we translate sijo, therefore, we should always bear in mind cultural differences. That is why we need cultural translation instead of word-by-word translation. Cultural translation enables us to avoid the mischaracterization of a text.

2. On Variations of the Sijo Format

The basic format of sijo is 3-4-4(3)-4; 3-4-4(3)-4; and 3-5-4-3. However, slight variations have always been permitted. The same thing goes for the translation of sijo, whether it is from Korean into English or from English into Korean. Variations are also allowed when translating ancient sijo written in classical Chinese characters to modern Korean. Especially in modern sijo, poets enjoy flexibility in format because creating sijo's poetic sensitivity is more important than following a fixed format.

Recently, I came across two insightful sijo poems written by Americans who won prizes in the sijo contest by the Sejong Cultural Society in Chicago. One was "Social Distancing" and the other was "In Middle School." Although written in English without faithfully following the format of sijo, the award-winning sijo poems have successfully captured the unique sensitivity and atmosphere of the traditional Korean poetic form.

"Social Distancing" by Julie Shute, is an excellent sijo that painfully captures the social milieu of the pandemic year 2020 when we shunned one another in order to avoid the coronavirus.

Neighborhoods bereft of neighbors. Teeming cities, bare.
We orbit our own lives. Joined in isolation. All, alone.
We see how our fates are interwoven, just as they unravel.

Ever since its outbreak, COVID-19 has disintegrated and degenerated our society by forcing us to avoid contact with others and put an end to our age-old beautiful custom of greeting and hugging. Consequently, we have lost the warmth of human touch in bone-chillingly inhumane modern cities. Hence, the first line of "Social Distancing" laments the barren landscape of our modern wasteland. Then the second line penetrates into our lonely predicament.

Tennessee Williams once said, "We are all sentenced to solitary confinement inside our own skins, for life." Nevertheless, we continue to interact and have rapport with others. Despite this complete isolation, however, the poet perceives that even though we are isolated in our own orbit, we have "joined in isolation."

Thus, Shute does not despair and explores a new possibility in the final line: "We see how our fates are interwoven, just as they unravel." Despite compulsory social distancing due to the pandemic, Shute perceives our "interwoven" fates and dreams of a new society where we can restore warm human touch at least in our heart, though it may be invisible.

"In Middle School" is written by a high school girl named Esther Kim; in her poem, Kim recollects her middle school years, touching upon a painful, compelling identity crisis that Asian immigrants in the US inevitably come to experience in their vulnerable adolescent years.

I thought that beauty meant
    discarding my Korean self.
I wished to leave my yellow skin,
    but my umma comforted me;
she said, "Yellow is the color
    of forsythias, bright and beautiful."

"In Middle School" painstakingly depicts the psychological conflicts of a minority teenage girl who finds that she is different from others. Situated on the border of her home country and host country, the Korean American girl wants to assimilate into mainstream American society by discarding her differences. In the fourth line, however, Kim deliberately chooses the Korean word, "umma" instead of "mom," acknowledging the importance of her Korean heritage. In fact, you do not need to "leave" your skin color or discard your Korean self in order to become an American. Instead, you can embrace your Korean heritage, be confident in it, and make the most of it. Ethnic or cultural differences have nothing to do with better or worse, or right or wrong. They have to do with variety and diversity. Gradually, the young poet realizes that her uniqueness and difference can be an advantage in a multiethnic, multicultural society such as America. Finally, she comes to understand that beauty lies in her Korean identity or in the combination of the two cultures she inherited.

In his celebrated novel *Yellow*, Korean American writer Don

Lee explored the possibilities of what it means to be Asian American by redefining the concepts of difference and identity. Lee does not perceive diasporic identity as a crisis. Rather, he embraces it as a new possibility. The final line of "In Middle School" echoes Lee: "Yellow is the color/ of forsythias, bright and beautiful." The teenage girl seems to have accepted her mom's advice and overcome her identity crisis because she has titled her poem "In Middle School".

The late Edward W. Said, a Palestinian American literary critic, called himself "a self-appointed exile." Despite being an exile on foreign soil, Said seldom grieved or harbored grudges. To the contrary, in his monumental book *Culture and Imperialism*, professor Said enlightens us: "Yet when I say exile, I do not mean something sad or deprived. On the contrary, belonging, as it were, to both sides of the imperial divide enables you to understand them more easily."

"In Middle School" reminds me of Said who must have had the same identity crisis as a spiritual exile in America. Indeed, it would be nice if Korean American teenagers, too, could have the confidence and open-mindedness of the late Said.

The above sijo poems provide a profound insight into how to be "joined in isolation" in difficult times. Surely, sijo is an excellent medium through which we can perceive our world better. The above sijo poems also remind me of the fact that we can write excellent sijo without adhering to the fixed format.

3. Sijo as a Means of Communication

In medieval Korea, poetry was often a medium of correspondence and communication among learned men. People addressed each other in poems and conveyed messages metaphorically in three- or four-line poems. The recipient of the correspondence would also reply with a terse poem. Westerners may find it hard to understand, but the power of poetry was so potent in Korea that it could win a lover's heart and even prevent war.

When General Wu of the Sui dynasty in China invaded Korea in A.D. 612, Korean General Eulji Mundeok sent a short poem to persuade him to withdraw. After reading the poem, the Chinese general surprisingly decided to give up the military campaign and pull back his troops to China. The anecdote is so famous because a short poem prevented the seemingly inevitable, imminent war. The famous four-line poem was as follows:

Your unfathomable strategy can reach heaven
Your intricate calculation can penetrate the earth
Winning so many battles already
You should know when to stop and withdraw.

It was neither a petition nor a threat, neither praise nor criticism. The message was so intricate and metaphoric that ordinary people could hardly understand the underlying meaning. Yet the Chinese warrior understood the poem and acted accordingly. It is amazing that even warriors used to address each other in poems. Perhaps General Wu did not have a choice except to pull back his troops due to the lack of supplies. Nevertheless, the poem from the Korean general surely prompted him to make the final decision (see Editor's note on page 100).

Another example of poems that resulted in historic events is the two famous sijo poems exchanged between Yi Bang-won and Jeong Mong-ju in the late Goryeo dynasty, at a time when sijo first appeared. In the late fourteenth century, the faltering Goryeo dynasty was challenged by the House of Yi that later founded the Yi dynasty. Yi Bang-won, who later became the third king of the Yi dynasty, invited Jeong Mong-ju, an influential minister of the Goryeo dynasty, to a feast to test his loyalty to the falling dynasty. Yi recited the following sijo poem (translated by Inez Kong Pai) to Jeong Mong-ju:

What difference does it make, this way or that?
The tangled vines of Mt. Mansu in profusion grow entwined
We too could be like that, and live together a hundred years.

To this tempting sijo poem, Jeong Mong-ju improvised the following sijo:

Though I may die, die a hundred times
Until my bones become dust and my spirit is gone
My loyalty to the kingdom will be everlasting.

Listening to this poem, Yi Bang-won gave up on Jeong Mong-ju. On his way back home, Jeong was ambushed and killed by the assassins sent by Yi. Before the tragic incident, Jeong's mother advised her son to stay away from conspiring politicians, once again through a sijo.

Do not go near a flock of crows, my white crane
Angry crows may be jealous of your white feathers
And stain your spotless body washed in the clean river.

In medieval times, Korean women, too, used sijo to express their feelings toward beloved ones. Hwang Chini, the most celebrated *kisaeng* (female entertainer) who lived in the sixteenth century, composed exquisite love poems. Since she was so charming and attractive, all the men fell in love with her as soon as they laid an eye on her, except a man named Byeok Kye-su (Crystal-clear Water). Thus, Hwang, whose pen name was Myongwol (Bright Moon), wrote a celebrated love sijo, playing with their symbolic names:

O crystal-clear water in the green mountain, do not boast of your speed
Once you reach the sea, never can you turn back again
How about come and rest while the bright moon shines over the mountain?

Im Je, a famous playboy in the sixteenth century wrote another romantic sijo. Visiting the celebrated *kisaeng* Han-wu (Cold Rain), Im Je metaphorically confessed his desire to stay overnight:

Clear was the Northern sky, and I came without an umbrella
Now a snowstorm hits the mountain and rain falls in the field
Soaked in cold rain, I must sleep icy cold tonight.

Then the warm-hearted, beautiful Han-wu replied also in sijo:

Why must you sleep icy cold, my dear?
We have this comfortable honeymoon bed here
Soaked in cold rain, you deserve warm sleep tonight.

These days, such intricate poetic sensibility seems to have disappeared from our society. Unlike our ancestors who practiced restraint, we have become too direct, too blunt, and too hasty. We no longer send poems to our beloved ones or to our enemies. Instead of sending poems, we ask rather bluntly, "Are you with us or not?" To our boyfriend or girlfriend, we ask directly, "Do you love me or not?" or "Can I stay over?" I miss those old days when people communicated with each other in sijo that brilliantly exhibited poetic subtlety and delicacy.

> *Editor's note:* There are two versions of the Battle of Salsu River and how General Eulji Mundeok's small army crushed the mighty and numerically superior Chinese army. Also, there are two versions of the Chinese general's response to Eulji Mundeok's poem. (see page 24)

Sijo Makes You Smarter

Linda Sue Park

I didn't learn about sijo until I was an adult. The path to sijo for me was a long and bumpy one.

My parents immigrated to the U.S. in the 1950s, right after the Korean War ended. My father arrived here in 1954, my mother in 1956. I grew up in the Chicago area, in Park Forest, a south suburb. We were the only Korean family in the whole town until I was eight years old. I have a clear memory of my mother's excitement when the second Korean family moved to town.

Maybe three or four times a year, we would drive an hour or so to Chicago, to the nearest Korean grocery store. The three of us kids had to be good and patient while my parents did the shopping. If we behaved ourselves, at the very end, at the checkout register, my father would buy us each a box of sweets, the kind with edible rice-paper wrappers that seemed magical to us.

My parents made the crucial decision not to speak Korean to us, so my siblings and I grew up speaking only English. That was very much in keeping with the times, when immigrants were supposed to assimilate as quickly as possible, and I think my parents believed that having English as our first language would help us with that process. Now, of course, I regret that I don't speak Korean, but I don't blame my parents. I know that they thought they were making the best decision at the time. Other than the language, I grew up with a lot of Korean culture in the home. Rice for dinner every night! And my parents always shared with us Korean values and traditions. I even gave my Irish husband a *hwan-gap* party when he turned sixty.

Although I grew up steeped in Korean cultural traditions, I knew very little about Korean history. Naturally, being a student in American schools, I learned American history. When I got pregnant with my first child, my husband and I were living in London. My husband is from Ireland, and we visited his family often; it was an easy trip from London to Dublin. So I knew my children would have the opportunity to learn about their Irish half. But what about the Korean side? There we were in London, far away from my family in the U.S.—how were they ever going to learn enough about being Korean?

I started getting books from the library and reading as much as I could about Korea and Korean history. And I started learning amazing things—things I had never known before. And suddenly, things about my childhood and my family began to make sense in a way that they hadn't before.

Here's one simple example. In our backyard, my brother and I used to jump up and down on this contraption my mother had made for us. It was very simple—just a plank of wood laid across a stout log. We had a great time on this thing, sending each other flying. It didn't occur to me at the time that I had never seen anything like it in anybody else's backyard.

Of course, what my mom had made for us was a Korean seesaw. Eventually I would read about it in Frances Carpenter's book *Tales of a Korean Grandmother.* And decades later, I would write my first book, called *Seesaw Girl.*

Here's another example. In my reading, I learned that during the Joseon era in Korea, there was only one way for a family to climb the social ladder. That was by passing the very difficult examinations to obtain a job as a civil servant. Families would make great sacrifices so that one of their children, almost always the oldest son, could study for those examinations. In exchange for not having to work or contribute to the family income, that child was expected to study very hard.

Hmmm...does this sound familiar? Suddenly my parents' attitude toward my grades had a historical context! Could it be at least a partial explanation for the fanatical emphasis most Korean-American families place on education? My interest in this topic led to my second book, *The Kite Fighters.*

Then I found out that during the Goryeo dynasty, Korean pottery was considered the finest in the world, so I wrote a book about that. *A Single Shard* was awarded the Newbery Medal in 2002, given by the American Library Association for the most distinguished contribution to U.S. children's literature.

I've written several other books with Korean themes or Korean American characters. But after I published my first few books, I started worrying about being pigeonholed. I loved learning about Korea and writing about it. But I also wanted to be free to write about any subject. I was worried that both publishers and readers would come to expect Korean books from me, and wouldn't be interested in any other kind of story I wrote.

So I wrote a picture book called *What Does Bunny See?* It's a rhyming story about a bunny hopping through a garden, learning colors and the names of flowers. This simple book might not seem like a fierce act of rebellion, but that's what it was for me. It opened a new door: I now felt that I could write about Korean topics and anything else I was interested in.

Again, going back to my research, I learned about a form of Korean poetry, sijo. When I first learned about sijo, I was delighted. It's a wonderful form, and I was immediately enchanted by it.

And then I got mad.

Everyone, it seems, knows about haiku. Students here in the U.S. learn about haiku in school. Haiku poems circulate on social media. They've become part of our cultural consciousness. Now, I like haiku, too, don't get me wrong. But I wondered why everyone knows about haiku, and almost no one knows about sijo. Sijo should be every bit as famous as haiku.

That was fifteen years ago or more. At the time, I found only two trade books of sijo in English, one for children and one for adults. The children's book was called *Sunset in a Spider Web*. The adult book is *Songs of the Kisaeng*. There were also some academic titles published by university presses. *Sunset in a Spider Web* was long out of print, which meant that there was no sijo collection for children available.

I decided to use the sijo form to write poems about topics with universal appeal to young readers. This was exciting for me—I would be combining a Korean tradition with contemporary American subject matter. It was the organic result of being liberated by the bunny book.

Tap Dancing on the Roof is illustrated by Istvan Banyai, who is Hungarian. In a very pleasing coincidence, it turns out that many linguists believe that the Korean and Hungarian languages might have a common root, both being in the Ural-Altaic family of languages. Here are two sijo from the book.

Summer Storm

Lightning jerks the sky awake to take its photograph, *flash!*
Which draws grumbling complaints or even tantrums from thunder—

He hates having his picture taken, so he always gets there late.

Breakfast

For this meal, people like what they like, the same each morning.
Toast and coffee. Bagel and juice. Cornflakes and milk in a white bowl.

Or—warm, soft, and delicious—a few extra minutes in bed.

I titled this talk, "Sijo makes you smarter." I believe that, and I'm going to explain why. Reading is a highly sophisticated skill. Decoding shapes into letters, letters into words, connecting the words to their meanings relative to the words around them—it's one of the most complicated things our brains have to do.

Reading poetry intensifies that experience because of its use of imagery. On top of the tasks listed above, the reader's brain also has to conjure images. And with short forms like sijo, our brains have very few words to work with. That makes reading sijo very interactive: We have to fill in those spaces ourselves, which enlarges our imaginations. We quite literally tap into brain cells that don't get used for other tasks. Stimulating those cells makes them available for creative connections in other realms of our lives. The ability to make those kinds of connections is the key to innovation and problem-solving. *Sijo makes you smarter.*

Poetry was my first love as a writer. As a young child, all the way through my teen years and college, I read and wrote poetry. I didn't begin writing fiction until I was in my late thirties. I've always been grateful that my first love was poetry because it has made me a better writer, and I truly believe that it's made me smarter.

There are a lot of ways to bring poetry into your daily lives. I subscribe to a free newsletter called The Slowdown. I get an email every day with a short poem. My husband subscribes, too. One of us will read the poem aloud to the other. I also keep poetry books in the bathroom. Seriously. At least once a day, you can take the opportunity to read a short poem.

I'm very grateful for the work of the Sejong Cultural Society. This kind of work is vital to the immigrant story. The Koreans who immigrated to this country along with my parents—that generation did not talk much about the past. My parents told me a few funny stories about growing up, but almost nothing about either World War II or the Korean War. The reasons are complicated, far-ranging, and difficult. But the result is that a whole generation—my generation—grew up knowing relatively little about the country of our ancestors.

We have been slow to learn that those stories are important. That they have to be shared. The erasure of a culture, whether by suppression, genocide, or benign neglect, has implications that echo for generations. In racism, subtle or blatant, from members of dominant cultures who believe that our silence means that our stories are insignificant. In family strife, when the struggle against the dominant culture corrodes our personal relationships as well. In myths such as the 'model minority,' which surrenders the power of self-definition to others, rather than allowing us to shape it ourselves.

Many people prefer to distance themselves from identity politics, but I have come to believe that when we do so, we are inviting others to ignore our culture, to arrive at the conclusion that it is unimportant to us. Efforts like the Sejong Cultural Society are vital for two reasons: to educate others, and to nurture pride among ourselves.

Since my publishing career began more than twenty years ago, I've seen the landscape change. For quite a long time, the Korean diaspora here in the U.S. tended to focus on fields where the language barrier would not be so daunting. Now, finally, Korean-Americans have gained confidence with English and are expressing themselves as writers. You can find articles with titles like "Five Korean Novels You Should Read Now," published in *Vanity Fair*. If you google 'Korean American authors', you'll find a list of several dozen names, which is very exciting!

I'm proud and happy to be working among such fine company, and I look forward to even greater numbers of writers and artists from the younger generations.

My latest book of poetry is called *The One Thing You'd Save*. It's a collection of connected poems set in a classroom. The teacher asks her students what one thing they would save if their home was on fire. Each poem is a response from a student as they consider, discuss, disagree, stick to their choices, and change their minds. The book closes with an author's note:

> For the poems in this collection, I have borrowed the line structure from sijo. A sijo (pronounced SHEE-zjo) is an ancient form of traditional Korean poetry. A classic sijo has three lines of about fourteen to sixteen syllables. Sometimes the three lines are divided into six shorter ones, seven to eight syllables each.
>
> The use of a consistent syllabic structure unites these poems in form as well as content. However, many of them are more than three lines long, which is definitely not traditional. Using old forms in new ways is how poetry continually renews itself, and the world.

Works Cited

Chung, Thomas. "Korean-American Writers List (Fiction, Poetry, Creative Non-Fiction, Memoir, Young Adult Fiction, Children's Fiction)". 2015. https://bit.ly/3xvCXAQ

Marcus, Lilit. "5 Korean Novels You Should Read Now". *Vanity Fair*, 2015. https://bit.ly/3lHsrEz

PART II

Sijo Lesson Plans

Sijo in an American Classroom:
Writing, Editing, Working Virtually and In-Person

Elizabeth Jorgensen

Creative Writing Teacher
Arrowhead Union High School, Hartland, Wisconsin

Each semester, I welcome 180 high school students to my creative writing classes with a course introduction and overview. When I say, "My goal is for each of you to be an award-winning or published author by the end of the semester," they look intrigued. I say, "Everything we do will be sent to a writers' market. This semester, you will practice what it means to be a professional author." What follows is a curriculum focused on submitting short stories, poems, and vignettes to competitions and publications.

I start with haiku, a familiar form of poetry.

"Oh yes, we did this in elementary school," a student says.

The Japanese haiku uses a five-seven-five syllable form and is typically about nature or the seasons. The class churns out haikus and submits them to various writers' markets.

"Now," I say, "if you can write haiku, you can write sijo, haiku's lesser-known Korean cousin." Students find comfort in the similarities. "And the thing about sijo is there's more flexibility—and more room to tell a story."

I learned about sijo a decade ago, but it's a Korean poetry

form older than haiku. Haiku poems are ubiquitous in American schools. The three-line, seventeen-syllable form introduces students to poetry and Japanese culture. Sijo is a logical progression from haiku: it is also East Asian, but longer, and can further challenge students to creatively think and write.

Sijo

When designing my poetry curriculum, I consider variety in both author and form. Since students know haiku, limerick, sonnet, and acrostic—and Robert Frost, Shel Silverstein, and Walt Whitman—I add new forms and poets. This challenges students to see what is possible within writing and to consider diversity in not only voice, but also in shape, sound, and style.

Sijo presents students with a structure for their stories and sijo's brevity (forty-four to forty-six syllables) easily fits into a curriculum.

At the beginning of the school year, the junior and senior students in my creative writing classes often struggle and feel intimidated; they don't identify as poets. Whether or not students view themselves as poets, they all have stories to tell, emotions to explore, and experiences to process. Poetry can be a vehicle for students to contribute their voice to the classroom, community, and canon.

Poetry has emotional and cognitive benefits: it demands precise language, requires attention to detail, builds empathy, and spurs creativity and analysis. Writing for authentic purposes, like the Sejong Cultural Society's sijo competition, gives students motivation. The competition also hosts a division for adults, which encourages teachers to write alongside students.

Using Inquiry

To prepare my students to write their own sijo, I share previous winning sijo to build an understanding that writing, like all art, is subjective; there are no right or wrong answers, no right or wrong responses. After reading each winning sijo poem, I ask questions. In their responses, my students discuss the value of art. Students analyze and decipher. They debate why poems may have won, why certain topics, language choices, or formats may have resonated with the judges. I ask questions to stimulate thoughts and to expand knowledge, understanding, and awareness.

- What is this poem about?
- What is the point of the poem?
- What emotions are evoked?
- Who are the characters?
- What is the setting?
- What is the twist?
- What do you think the title refers to—both before and after the twist?
- What stylistic devices do you notice?
- What parts of the poem are particularly beautiful?
- What tense does the author use? Why does she make this choice?
- What works for you in this poem?
- Where are you confused?
- What don't you like?

From here, I share more winning sijo, often ones my own students wrote. I read each poem aloud three times. To connect my students to the text, I remind them each was crafted by an author who made a series of intentional choices. Knowing these poems were written by students their own age builds confidence and resolve. Students read the poems and say, "If they can do it, I can too."

After we have read several poems, I ask students to explain what they notice. With each question, I aim to develop sensitivity, awareness, analysis, and critical thinking.

- How does the poem feel like a song?
- Why do you think the author wrote about this topic?
- What does this author suggest about life, about the universe?
- Who are the characters?
- What do you notice about the point of view?
- What literary devices are used?

Through dissection, students recognize the components of a successful sijo: story, characters, plot, emotion, beauty, art, and song. Students notice the sijo is short and includes a twist. They identify topics to explore when they write their own.

In analyzing exemplars, using the winning poems as mentor texts, and answering my questions, students begin to see their world more vividly, more consciously. They recognize the stories in their lives—waiting to be shared, to be written about, to be crafted into art.

Responding to Sijo

One example I use to probe students' reactions is a 2016 honorable mention in the Sejong Cultural Society's annual competition:

Untitled
by Katie McFarland

Here I am, the human pincushion, constantly stabbing my skin with needles.
Here I am, a disappointment to my parents, with a chronic disease.
Here I am, a teenager, trying to hold onto a piece of nonexistent string.

I ask brave students to share what is most personal to them. I reference McFarland's poem and we discuss how her experiences and emotions are universal. I ask students who they are afraid to disappoint, if they have a piece of string to hold on to. I ask if they think McFarland's chronic disease is physical. I also ask why McFarland repeated "Here I am" three times. There are no right answers to any of my questions. My classroom becomes a writers' community—students relying on each other, noticing each other's responses, making connections, and hearing perspectives.

CHOOSING A TOPIC

To weave sijo into a curriculum, students could write from their own or someone else's perspective. Students in a parenting class could write from the point of view of a child, childcare worker, grandparent, or sibling. In social studies, students could narrate a poem as a prince or a member of the bourgeoisie. In art, students could explore the perspective of a painting or a famous artist—or write a sijo instead of a traditional artist statement.

In 2019, the second place poem in the Sejong Cultural Society's sijo competition considered the point of view of a female outcast, forced to entertain the upper class. In composing this poem, Hye In Lee imagined a different experience, during a different time, for a different person. Her sijo encouraged readers to empathize with and understand a woman born into a predetermined fate. She said, "I've sought to incorporate Korean culture into my poetry and wanted to write from the perspective of a woman in Korean history. I came across the stories of the *kisaeng*, who often dealt with the sijo style, and thought it would be interesting to write a sijo from a *kisaeng*'s perspective."

A Kisaeng's Sijo
by Hye In Lee

With the rhythm of the janggu, we dance like magpies,
iridescent and spinning, hoping for freedom from the men
and their hands feeling at our ivory ankles, calves, and thighs.

Dante Kirkman, an eighth grade student from Palo Alto, California, received an honorable mention in 2016 for his sijo.

Back in New Orleans
by Dante Kirkman

In the South, Grandpa was born. Paper shack house had a dirt floor.
As a kid he drank coffee. Milk for them was too expensive.
They were rich with gospel spirit! In church they sang, and filled their hearts.

Kirkman said, "My inspiration for the sijo poem was my grandfather, who grew up in segregated New Orleans during the Great Depression with nothing but his faith in God and a resolve to make a better life. After serving in World War II in the Philippines, he settled in San Francisco and made a life for his young family in Menlo Park, California, on the red-lined Black side, east of the freeway. He worked as a mailman and raised five children, and now I am honoring his legacy as his grandson, and my older brother is the first to go to college."

I prompt students to write about topics they are interested in and say, "You can write about anything in your sijo. And if you're writing about something you find enjoyable, it's more likely the reader will enjoy your piece too. Your passion will seep through."

When introducing a new topic, form or skill, I coax students with compliments and encouragement. I remind students that although there is a form to the sijo, like all art, they are in control.

Peer Editing

Students share drafts with peer editing partners, small groups, and the whole class. During peer editing, I provide a worksheet (see end of this chapter) to guide students.

Putting it Together

I compose alongside my students, showing how messy my process and how imperfect my art. I model how writing works: slowly, creatively, through trial and error. We are a community of learners wading through drafting, writing, and editing.

I share my feelings about submitting to the Sejong Cultural Society's adult sijo competition. Then, I encourage students to submit their own sijo to a variety of writers' markets. Students enter the Sejong Cultural Society's annual competition; I create a class book of sijo; students send sijo to their mom, dad, grandpa, auntie, best-friend, and boyfriend. We enjoy the best part of creating, of being artists: sharing our work with others. Another possibility for collaborating and celebrating is a poetry night or classroom bulletin board.

By the end of our time together, my students not only believe their voices are worthy of publication, but they also begin to identify as writers and poets. Students tell me they enjoy the process of learning a new form, of using discussion and inquiry, of writing for an authentic purpose.

Writing and submitting poems to writers' markets allows students to contribute to the canon. This also helps students realize the purpose of writing: to connect, entertain, inform, process, persuade, explain. To enjoy.

Although all students struggle as they learn and grow and write, through sijo, they expand not only what they know about language, but also what they know about themselves, their classroom, their community, and their world.

From Inception to Award: Helping Students Edit Sijo

The sijo-writing process involves multiple drafts that are edited (both by peer editors and me) and then revised. This method has proven successful in improving the quality of student writing. It has also resulted in publication and awards for students.

Students share documents with me electronically. After each draft, I give students my genuine, emotional response to their art.

On first and second drafts, I encourage. Allowing students to believe they possess skills is the first step—part of my prescription to help them overcome anxiety, writer's block, and doubt. Positivity also fosters my relationship with students.

On third and fourth drafts, I ask questions about word choice and punctuation to help students consider the choices they've made and their impact on a reader.

- Is this what you intended?
- What titles are you considering?
- Is there another action verb you could use?
- What stylistic device might help your poem sing?
- What line are you most proud of?
- Where are you struggling?
- What are you unhappy with?
- What emotion do you want to evoke in this piece?
- What do you think the point of this story is?
- What do you want the reader to take away?
- What about adding X, Y, or Z?
- Is there a better word to use here?
- How can you elevate the poetic nature of this piece?

FROM INCEPTION TO AWARD: ERIN VANEVENHOVEN

Erin, a junior, sits at her desk with her laptop and journal. "I'm not sure what I want to write about."

She and the other students in her high school class brainstorm topics for a sijo for the Sejong Cultural Society's annual competition. Erin and her classmates read previous winning poems on the competition's website and a book of sijo: *Tap Dancing on the Roof* by Linda Sue Park.

In her sijo, Erin can choose her own topic; and I've encouraged each student to tackle something they care about. Some students explore a passion or experience (playing soccer or being asked to prom); others decide to play with words (telling a joke or using irony); others want to craft a fictional story.

Erin turns to her peer editing partner and says, "I haven't decided if I want to do something with a lot of emotion or if I want to do something more mundane, but I might do something about talking about my grandmother and use present tense and the twist is that I never got to remember a time when she was here. Maybe something to that effect."

I'm pleased Erin perceived how Park and previous winning student poets used present tense to engage readers. But I'm even more encouraged by her topic choice.

"Erin," I say, "it sounds like you share a special bond with your family. If you use this as your inspiration, your poem would be a wonderful tribute to what your family members mean to you. Keep thinking; you're on the right track."

Throughout the semester I encourage Erin, as I do with all students, to focus on passions and skills—and not on grades or areas of weakness.

During the sijo unit, Erin spends at least two weeks (brainstorming, writing, editing, sharing, polishing) before submitting a final draft. Throughout the unit, students and I dialogue and discuss (both in person and electronically), working together to improve the sijo. During class, I connect with struggling or eager students. Outside of class, students share electronic documents for individual feedback. Students and I go back and forth, until we collaboratively decide their sijo is ready for the competition.

In the first draft, I suggest students tell a story. I don't want students to get bogged down by the format or word choice. I say, "Just write your first line as the introduction, the second line as the development, and the third line as the twist and conclusion. We can work on syllables, word choice, and editing later."

Erin submits a draft:
An Infant opens her eyes, takes her first breath, speaks her first sound
A mother forgets the pain she feels. Her pain masked-for now.
Couldn't cancer wait one more day? This baby will not meet her grandpa.

In my first round of feedback, I hope to stimulate progress through compliments and praise. To Erin, I write, "You have a great poem! You're telling a story, it's emotional, and you successfully use the present tense."

I then move line by line:

- "What about a title?"
- "In the first line, I notice you're not using complete sentences, intentional capitalization, or punctuation. Can you go through the poem and make sure each choice is intentional?"
- I also ask Erin about the pain in the second line. "How can you show this? What does it feel like?"
- In the third line, I ask Erin to consider the character and why she refers to the baby as "she" in previous lines, but as "This baby" in the third.

After looking at my feedback, Erin makes edits and comes up

with this:

One More Day

An infant opens her eyes, takes her first breath, speaks her first sound;
a mother stifles sorrow. Her pain is masked—momentarily.
One more day—couldn't cancer wait?   She will never meet grandpa.

On my second round of feedback, I again start with praise:

- "I love the language choices and the scene you're setting."
- "Powerful storytelling."
- "Nice update editing punctuation. You're successfully using the em dash and semicolon now."

I notice Erin has added punctuation to the first line. In the second line, she removed the extra spaces, added a dash and semicolon and used alliteration. In the third line, she's used a different question and conclusion.

To improve the poem, I ask Erin to look at the verbs.

- "Can you use an action verb rather than 'is'?"
- "What do you think about the word 'will'?"

I also direct Erin to note the syllables in each line. This will help me double-check the sijo form.

Knowing when to provide praise and when to provide constructive criticism is a delicate task and varies from student to student. I want to empower students, yet I also want them to experience the rigor and demands of quality writing. In each round of feedback I provide, I aim for more positives than negatives. Students also seem to respond to questions better than statements; it allows them, as the writer, to take control of their craft.

Erin adds syllables and shares her draft with a peer editing partner.

One More Day

An infant opens her eyes, takes her first breath, speaks her first sound;

3-4-4-4 (15)

a mother stifles sorrow. Her pain is masked—momentarily.

3-4-4-5 (16)

One more day—couldn't cancer wait? She will never meet grandpa.

3-5-4-3 (15)

(45)

Her partner says, "You could delete 'a' and capitalize Mother. Then go over to where it says: Her pain is...and erase the period and put the word 'and' in. Delete 'is' and then you still have the same syllables with a complete sentence."

The syllables I asked Erin to include help her partner double check the form. Her partner suggests "for a moment" rather than "momentarily." This helps Erin stick to the sijo form by ending the second line with four syllables instead of five. Her partner also suggests a change to the ending: "An infant without a grandpa."

I am excited by Erin's thought and care and I want to encourage her progress, so I email her parents:

Hello Mr. and Mrs. Vanevenhoven,

I hope you're doing well!

I have Erin in Creative Writing. She is currently working on a sijo. Erin is doing awesome things in the poem and I just wanted to let you know how impressed I am with her initial draft. If you're interested, ask her to share the draft with you. I hope you are as impressed by it as I am.

I am sure the draft will only get better as she continues to work.

Have a great day!

Liz :)

Erin takes another day to work with the poem and shares this with me:

One More Day

An infant opens her eyes, takes her first breath, speaks her first sound;
a mother stifles sorrow and masks her pain for a moment.
One more day—couldn't cancer wait? An infant, without a grandpa.

I read the poem a couple of times to absorb the changes and progress. I am pleased with Erin's ability to use stylistic devices and varied punctuation and elevate her piece through revision, peer editing, and our collaboration.

I say, "Erin, I like all the 's' sounds: speaks sound, stifles sorrow. I also really like how you've used the word infant at the beginning and at the end of the poem. The use of varied punctuation also sticks out; you've used the semicolon, the dash, and a question mark. The present tense is effective and the emotion is strong and powerful. I like the characters and setting and I'm really pleased with this poem if you are."

After reading a book of sijo, looking at previous winning poems on the Sejong Cultural Society's webpage, and working through editing, drafting, three rounds of feedback, and a peer editing session, Erin agrees the poem is complete.

Erin submits to the Sejong Cultural Society's sijo competition. When the results are announced, Erin receives an honorable mention and $50; but she's not the only one. Another student,

Kaitlyn Laufenberg, also receives an honorable mention for her poem:

Family Arguments

My grandpa hosts a cramped Christmas, with four kids and six grandkids.
When they visit, fourteen strong voices bicker at one another.
In silence, Grandpa smiles. Everyone he loves is here.

Kaitlyn says, "This competition pushed my creativity. I am so grateful...to have been part of this competition!"

In addition to the Sejong Cultural Society, students submit sijo to other writers' markets, including *Teen Ink*. Two students, Margaret Newman and Jaron Luther, receive Editors' Choice Awards:

Untitled
by Margaret Newman

The house stills—your presence, gone. No caresses against my spine.
Without you—sickening silence. I'm sorry—I overlooked you.
The shuddering curtain stills; the house shifts to sleep.

The Beautiful Fight
by Jaron Luther

Brain cancer slowly gives her less, steals her electrifying life.
Her pranks, her conversations, her control, her fight.
A living reminder, our angel—protects, rises, and gives us more.

Throughout the semester, I find more writers' markets for students to submit sijo and I share successes with school administrators. The superintendent posts congratulations on our school's Facebook page. The associate principal sends each student an email, including this one to Erin: "How did you get so talented! I enjoyed reading your work and am so proud of your accomplishments! WRITE ON!"

At the end of the semester, I ask Erin to reflect on her progress. She says, "We have completed many writing pieces over this semester, but one of them stands out the most to me which was the sijo poem and the competition. I had such a fun time writing this piece because it didn't leave any question about the format I was supposed to use, but I was able to be creative and think more broadly for words I could use to fit into the syllable count. I also really enjoyed the poem because my mom was really touched by it and called and sent it to all of my aunts and uncles who began to tear up when they heard it. Without this class, none of that would have happened and I am very grateful for that."

From Inception to Award: Trace Morrissey

Over the course of two weeks, Trace Morrissey, a senior, works with his peer editing partner and me to compose and submit his sijo.

Trace starts by reading and reflecting on *Tap Dancing on the Roof* by Linda Sue Park and other winning poems on the Sejong Cultural Society's webpage. After reading example sijo, he says,

- "Sijo can be literally about anything. I can fit many poetic devices in a sijo."
- "While reading, if I pause in the correct places, based on punctuation, it sounds better and more meaningful."
- "I think Linda Sue Park chose to punctuate poems on how she wanted the reader to read the poem. She used different punctuation in 'Breakfast' because there were many pauses; she used three lines. But in 'Crocuses,'

there were minimal pauses and the poem read more like a long sentence; she used six lines. 'Breakfast' sounded most like a song for me. I thought it sounded like a slower, sad song. It has pauses, but it still flows really well. I am going to use three lines and pauses."

- "I am going to write a sijo that has a sad twist, so I can really try to evoke an emotion. I am a little worried about making sure I have the correct amount of syllables while at the same time making my poem flow and evoke an emotion."

Trace shares his first draft with me and I provide comments on his electronic document.

Trace—Version One

I have not seen him in almost two years. I could not wait. We always stayed out late.
The air felt lighter when he was home, the food tasted better, music sounded more upbeat.
My brother exited the plane, in a pine wood box, covered in an American flag. I guess he was home for good.

My Comments—Version One

- "I like the topic choice. It's clear you're using emotion and telling a story that is important to you and has a point. I like the characters, setting, and plot. Nice work!"
- "Now, you need to get the poem to be closer to a sijo. To condense, consider what is most important in each line. Focus on using the correct amount of syllables to make the poem a sijo. Remove what isn't essential to the story. Example: In line one, is it important that you stayed out late?"

- "Action verbs remain the core of quality writing. In line one, what action verb could you use?"
- "Also, look at the verb in line two—can you remove 'was' and instead use action verbs?"
- "In line one, who is the 'we'? Is that the right pronoun?"
- "What's the strongest part of the last line? How can you use that focus as your conclusion?"

Trace—Version Two

Not seeing him in two years, anxious to be together.
Air felt lighter, food tasted better, music sounded upbeat.
He is now home, in pine wood box, covered in an American flag.
Or
My brother left the plane, in a pine wood box, covered in an American flag. He is now home.

My Comments—Version Two

- "Nice work condensing each line. The poem is much easier to read."
- "Can you focus on using complete sentences now? That will help the reader digest your story. Specifically, line one trips me up. Who is the character who hasn't seen 'him'?"
- "In line two, nice action verbs: felt, tasted, sounded! Good job removing what wasn't necessary in that line. I also like the rule of thirds you're using in the list. Good sensory details."
- "Can you check the syllables and make sure each line has the correct groupings and total?"
- "Have you thought about a title?"
- "Anxious means nervous and you make it sound like

the emotion should actually be eager in line one. Thoughts?"
- "I wonder if there is a way to combine the best parts of each line you have before and after the Or?"

Trace—Version Three

Coming home

Not seeing my brother in two years, I remain eager.
Air felt lighter, food tasted better, music more upbeat, sun brighter.
But he came home in a plane, in a pine box, covered in a flag.

My Comments—Version Three

- "Overall, quality verbs, successful showing, and a powerful, emotional conclusion."
- "The title works for me! It doesn't give too much away, yet it alludes to your topic. I like how you use the word 'home' in your title and at the end of your poem."
- "Great use of a complete sentence in the first line."
- "The alliteration is also nice: music more; he came home; plane in a pine."
- "In the first line, you use the present tense. Is this what you intended to use? Line two and three use past tense."
- "I think 'eager' works better than 'anxious.'"
- "I also really like what you've done in the third line. Good pacing with the punctuation."
- "This feels like a sijo. I also like 'but' as the turn that starts the twist in the third line."
- "I think you're ready to share this draft with your peer editing partner; see what he thinks!"

Peer Editing Partner's Comments—Version Three

- "I think Trace's sijo is well written. I think his title is very relevant, but at the same time does not reveal too much information about the poem. His poem feels like a country song. I like the verbs in line two the best: felt, tasted. His verbs help the reader know about the character through the feel of the air, the taste of the food, and the sound of the music. Since that's my favorite part, could that start the poem? I feel that it works with what's going on."

My Comments—Post Peer Editing

- "I agree with your peer editing partner. Do you want to try moving around the lines?"

Trace—Version Four, Final Draft

Coming home
by Trace Morrissey, 12th grade honorable mention 2020

Air felt lighter, food tasted better, music more upbeat, sun brighter.
Not seeing my brother in two years, I remained eager.
But he came home in a plane, in a pine box, covered in a flag.

My name is Trace Morrissey and I am currently a senior at Arrowhead High School. Once I graduate, I am enlisting in the Air Force with the end goal of becoming a pilot. During my free time, I like to spend time outdoors with friends. I also enjoy going up north to spend time on a lake, or skiing. One person who has always been my hero is my grandpa. He taught me so much about life and how to treat people respectfully. Although we lost him in November 2019, I feel as if he is still teaching me lessons today. I learned while writing my sijo I needed to connect with the reader and to trigger an emotion. Since I have learned this, my writing has drastically improved. My inspiration for writing this poem came from a Vietnam War veteran that came and spoke with our class one day. He talked about how he lost good friends in the war and how he cannot forget some of the things he saw while fighting. We also wrote letters in class to veterans going on the Honor Flight. Most people wrote back and those who did had an impact on everyone who read their response.

CONCLUSION

Students are often resistant to editing, but inquiry and compliments allow me to understand each student's process as well as remind students we are in this together.

Sijo Poem//Peer Editing Worksheet

POET:
EDITOR:
STORY AND TWIST. Explain the following:
> Plot:
> Twist:
> Setting:
> Character(s):
> The point of the poem:
> Where are you confused?
> What is the best part of the story/poem? Why?

LANGUAGE CHOICES. Which stylistic devices does the author use? Please note each stylistic device and the impact on the reader. Please note at least three.
> 1.
> 2.
> 3.

What action verbs are present?

Where can the author insert a stylistic device, improve the language, or use action verbs? Give two suggestions:

SYLLABLES. Notate each line's syllable groupings. Example: 3-4-4-4
> Line one:
> Line two:
> Line three:
> Line four:
> Line five:
> Line six:

Count the total number of syllables in the poem. Place it here:

SONG. How is your partner's sijo like a song?

What could your partner do to make it *more* like a song?

TITLE. Current title:
Comment on the title and/or give a recommendation for improvement:

REFLECT. Overall, what do you think of your partner's sijo? Write four to six sentences.

NOW, read your peer editing partner's comments. THEN, go back to your sijo and make updates based on your partner's feedback. After this hour, I will look for an updated draft of your sijo.

Teaching Sijo Virtually

In addition to teaching sijo face-to-face, I have also taught sijo remotely using a variety of learning management systems.

Learning the Form

I start by asking students to explore the sijo form. Students independently read the following:
https://www.sejongculturalsociety.org/resources/resources.php

- "A Basic Guide to Writing Sijo".
- Gyung-ryul, Jang. (2016). "In search of the essence of sijo." *Korean Literature Now*, 31(1), 34-37.
- McCann, David. "The Sijo, A Window into Korean Culture." *Education About Asia*, Volume 15, Number 1, Spring 2010.
- Jorgensen, Elizabeth. "Korean Poetry Competition Provides Opportunity for American Creative Writing Students." *Wisconsin English Journal*, Volume 58, Number 2, Fall 2016.
- Jorgensen, Elizabeth. "Sijo: Power in Diversity." *Teachers, Profs, Parents: Writers Who Care*.

Students watch the following:

- The Sejong Cultural Society's YouTube channel.
  https://www.youtube.com/user/KoreanTheme
  - There are videos for both primary and secondary students.
  - Students appreciate being able to pause or re-watch sections; they also get to see a variety of approaches

to sijo.
- Professor Mark Peterson's video on YouTube channel, *The Frog Outside the Well*. https://bit.ly/3ENbONA
- My own lectures on sijo.

The articles and recordings allow students to build a knowledge base. After reading and watching, students post to discussion boards, pose questions, make connections, and reflect on what they learned. I offer virtual office hours for students who need additional explanation or assistance.

Exploring the Competition and Reading Student Examples

Once students comprehend the sijo form, I direct them to *Sijo Competition Rules and Information* on the Sejong Cultural Society's webpage; there, students read and analyze previous winning sijo.

When students read previous winning poems, they begin to see what is possible. They also notice what they like or want to do in their own poems.

I ask students to read at least ten different poems and tell me what they noticed using the following format: I read (title) by (author), (year), and I thought or noticed (three specific things).

Students post reflections to a discussion board. This builds community and allows students to connect with one another; it also allows students to dive deeper into analyzing previous winning poems.

When students post to discussion boards, set clear expectations: number of words, proper grammar, reply format. Discussion boards build classroom dialogue; they allow each student to participate and contribute to the virtual space.

STUDENT EXAMPLES

I read *Heaven* by Emmanuelle Sasson, 2019, and I noticed/thought...
- The author presented existential concepts.
- The author used bright imagery and beautiful word choice.
- There was a cool twist at the end.

I read *A Kisaeng's Sijo* by Hye In Lee, 2019, and I noticed/thought...
- What is the historical context?
- What are all the cultural references?
- What is the bigger meaning?

I read *Untitled* by Dorthea Kuemmerle, 2019, and I noticed/thought...
- I enjoyed the meadow imagery and the use of the senses on the spring day.
- I enjoyed how the end twists into a piano concert.
- I think this poem is about getting trapped in your own work.

I read *Abandoned* by Lily Daniels, 2019, and I noticed/thought...
- There is clear imagery.
- She uses a question to leave me thinking at the end. The question makes me wonder what happened.
- Whose life is she talking about?

I read *Absentee Parents* by Sofia Liaw, 2019, and I noticed/thought...
- The first sentence shows the relationship between the character and their parents.
- The poem tells the reader what skills she has learned.
- Sofia uses imagery in all lines.
- I found the poem to be both inspirational and motivational.

I read *The Forever Game* by Kate Dorazio, 2019, and I noticed/thought...
- The dialogue makes me think about what my own response would be.
- The poem gives me an idea of how the author was in high school.
- It was motivational.

I read *One More Day* by Erin Vanevenhoven, 2019, and I noticed/thought...
- Erin uses the senses (sight, touch) in her sijo.
- Erin uses imagery.
- The sijo gives me a feeling of warmth and love.
- The use of different kinds of punctuation makes the writing complex.

READING PROFESSIONAL EXAMPLES

Students then read *Tap Dancing on the Roof* by Linda Sue Park and complete the following worksheet.

Tap Dancing on the Roof//Reflection Worksheet

1. Please explain what you learned about sijo from reading Tap Dancing on the Roof.
   a.
   b.
   c.
   d.

2. Which were your favorite sijo?
   a. I enjoyed "insert title" because
   b. I enjoyed "insert title" because
   c. I enjoyed "insert title" because

3. Park wrote sijo in both three and six lines. Please explain why or how you think she chose six or three lines for her structure. Reference specific sijo by title.

4. Which sijo had the strongest rhythm/beat/pattern? In other words, which sijo felt most like a song? Explain why you thought this and reference specific sijo by title.

5. Which twists did you like best? Why?

6. Comment on Park's titles. What did you notice?

7. What did you notice about Park's punctuation and capitalization? Reference specific sijo by title.

8. List ten of Park's best action verbs:

9. List at least three of Park's best stylistic devices and explain why you liked them.

10. Where does Park break the sijo structure? Why do you think she does this? Why might this be acceptable? Reference specific sijo by title.

11. Reflect on sijo. How do you feel about writing your own? What are you thinking? What are you still wondering?

Brainstorming

Reading both student and professional sijo gives students a knowledge base to begin their own. I ask students to post their sijo ideas on a discussion board. I give the following prompts:

- What story are you thinking of telling in your sijo?
- What might your characters, setting, and twist be?
- What is the point of your sijo?
- Why do you want to tell this story?
- How did the readings, videos, and previous winning sijo impact your decision?

Students' posts allow me insight; they also provide me with an opportunity to reach out to struggling students or to affirm progress.

Discussion boards connect students with one another and me. When working online, consider having students use web tools; some students will want to make videos, record audio, upload clips, or use animation in addition to (or instead of) posting text.

Writing and Editing

After the exploration, discussion and brainstorm phases,

students write individual drafts in Google Documents and share links on a discussion board. I tell students it is helpful to include syllable counts at the end of each line, as well as the total number of syllables in each poem.

Both the students and I provide feedback using the editing tools in Google Documents and in the space on the discussion board.

Students compose at least three drafts and receive at least three rounds of feedback from their classmates and me. Senior Josie Salzman said, "Coming from a person who was never confident about writing and didn't like to read, this way of feedback was very positive, encouraging, and helpful."

SUBMITTING

After several drafts are complete, students send sijo to a variety of writers' markets. Students also reflect on the progress they made and what they learned.

Junior Amber Thomas said, "Previously I hated poetry; I didn't understand it and thought it was always too metaphorical but now that I have had the opportunity to write my own sijo I actually like how they have turned out and I appreciate the art much more."

CONCLUSION

Sijo lends itself easily to virtual learning. There are electronic resources students can reference at their own pace; and in a virtual format, students have ample time to write, draft, and incorporate feedback.

When I teach sijo virtually, I post procedures clearly, return feedback in a timely manner, and provide discussion and collaboration opportunities. I keep students on task with daily or weekly deadlines, but I also remain flexible. To better reach students, I offer one-on-one live chats and video conferences. Although teaching online presents challenges, students have responded positively to virtual sijo units because they have time and space to be creative.

Previous versions of this chapter originally appeared in the following:

"Inquiry, Questioning and the Art of Korean Poetry." *Ohio Journal of English Language Arts*. Volume 59, No. 1. Summer/Fall 2019.
  https://bit.ly/3rXSHLW

"Korean Poetry Competition Provides Opportunity for American Creative Writing Students." *The Wisconsin English Journal*. Volume 58, Number 2. Fall 2016.
https://bit.ly/3AkRqS3

"Sijo: Power in Diversity." *Teachers, Profs, Parents: Writers Who Care*, 3 Feb. 2020.
https://bit.ly/2VGDAKw

"Teaching Poetry With Student Exemplars." *Edutopia*, George Lucas Educational Foundation, 23 Apr. 2020.
https://bit.ly/2VBtr23

Sijo Lesson Plan for Elementary School Students

Elizabeth Jorgensen

Creative Writing Teacher

The following is the teacher outline for *Sijo Lesson Series for Elementary School Students* which can be found on the Sejong Cultural Society's YouTube channel.

https://bit.ly/3jPtDTR

In four video clips, students
1) learn how to say sijo, what makes the sijo unique, as well as the form and function of each line;
2) read and analyze sijo written by professional and student poets;
3) prepare to write a sijo (consider a topic, setting, character, purpose, and twist); share sijo ideas and receive feedback

from classmates; and

4) take turns reading sijo and giving critiques.

Before using this lesson plan, familiarize yourself with sijo using the resources in this book and watch *Sijo Lesson Series for Elementary School Students*.

LESSON PLAN

- We are going to be learning about sijo. It's a type of poetry. What do you know about poetry?
  - It tells a story.
  - It has characters, setting, plot.
  - It's exciting or interesting to read.
  - It's art and beautiful.
- Sijo is a type of poetry from Korea.
- Practice saying "she-jo."
- There are a few things we need to know about sijo:
  - They are meant to be songs.
    - What do you know about songs?
    - Why do we listen to songs?
  - A sijo can have either three or six lines.
    - Today, we are going to write sijo in three lines.
  - Each line of a sijo has a set number of syllables.
  - What are syllables?
  - Practice counting syllables. Clap out syllables or use your hand and chin.
  - Each line in the three-line sijo has a different purpose.
    - The first line introduces the story,
    - the second line develops the story, and
    - the third line has a twist and conclusion.
      - How would you define a twist?
        - Surprise, something unexpected, an opposite.
  - Read sijo from *Tap Dancing on the Roof* by Linda

Sue Park.
- ■ "From the Window"
- ■ "Laundry"
- ■ "Shower"
  - ○ Discuss each poem.
    - ■ What is the sijo about?
    - ■ What is the twist?
    - ■ Who are the characters?
- Now you will write your own sijo, but first you need an idea. You will use the *Sijo Planning* worksheet to explore a topic.
- Now that worksheets are complete, share your ideas.
- Put your story idea into the sijo format using the *Sijo's Three Lines* worksheet.
- Share your sijo rough draft.
  - ○ These are only rough drafts, so as you read, consider updates you can make.
  - ○ Be prepared to provide your classmates with feedback (both compliments and suggestions for improvement).
- For homework, make updates to your sijo.
  - ○ Share your poem with a grown up or friend.
  - ○ Ask them what you can do to make your poem better.
- Tomorrow we will submit your poem to the Sejong Cultural Society's sijo competition and publish your sijo on our classroom bulletin board.

Download worksheets from https://bit.ly/3yQyTwx

Sijo Planning

What will your story be about?	Where will your story take place? Draw a picture.
Who are your characters? Give them names, ages, and a description.	Why do you want to tell this story?
What is your twist?	Draw something that represents your idea.

Sijo's Three Lines

Each line needs 14-16 syllables and 44-46 syllables total. Above each word, write the syllable count.

In the first line, introduce your story. Think about what your characters are doing and where they are. What do you want to say in your first line? (14-16 syllables)

In the second line, go deeper into your story. Think about what is happening and why you're telling this story. What do you want to say in your second line? (14-16 syllables)

In the third line, include a twist. Think about something that is unexpected or surprising or a change. What do you want to say in your last line? (14-16 syllables)

Sijo: Why Teaching Korean Poetry Matters in a History Class

Deborah Holland

High School History Teacher
D'Evelyn High School, Denver, Colorado

ABSTRACT

Learn how the Korean sijo transcends time by connecting history to the modern day. Students learn Korean history and express their creativity through this clever, simple, and engaging poetic form.

OBJECTIVES

Students will learn the background of this poetry form by reading sijo that carry the voices of historical figures and events. Students will be provided the opportunity to enter a national competition administered by the Sejong Cultural Society, in collaboration with the Korea Institute at Harvard University. Students will have the opportunity to win monetary awards and be published, should their sijo be selected as first, second, or third place, or an honorable mention.

Through the study and use of historical sijo students will be able to

- develop a deeper understanding of historical events through a unique literary format
- evaluate historical themes via primary documents
- enhance their understanding of Korean history and its people
- evaluate the position of various historical personas and perspectives in Korean society
- make connections to the purpose and spread of sijo today

By writing their own sijo, students will be able to

- learn the format and structure of sijo
- share their voices and express their creativity through a more than 700-year-old poetry form
- have the opportunity to share their sijo by entering a national writing competition
- connect cross-curricular content between a social studies lesson and literature in English language arts
- recognize and reflect on contemporary themes expressed in poetry that are similar to or different from historical themes
- engage in an interactive activity that will increase understanding of Korean culture, history, and literature
- participate in a discussion that fosters critical thinking

Teachers and students will have the opportunity to enter sijo in a national competition sponsored by the Sejong Cultural Society.

- The Sejong Cultural Society strives to "advance awareness and understanding of Korea's cultural heritage amongst people in the United States by reaching out to the younger generations through contemporary creative and fine arts."

- The goal of the Sejong Writing Competition is to "discover children and young adults talented in writing and to encourage them to learn and write about Korea and its culture."
- The Sejong Writing Competition is supported in part by grants from the Illinois Arts Council, Korea Foundation, Literature Translation Institute of Korea, the Daesan Foundation, the Doosan Yonkang Foundation, and the Academy of Korean Studies.
- Prizes are awarded to first, second, and third place winners of the sijo competition as well as honorable mentions. The winning entries are published in *Azalea: Journal of Korean Literature and Culture*, published by the Korea Institute at Harvard University. Winners' works may be published in the *Korea Times Chicago* or in the *Korean Quarterly*.
- For more information visit The Sejong Cultural Society website. http://sejongculturalsociety.org/

By the end of the lesson, students will be able to
- explain the impact of sijo on the Korean people, both historically and in modern times
- recognize the role sijo has played within Korean society and outside Korea
- use the exploration of writing sijo as a means to extend their voices
- construct a more perceptive understanding of their thoughts and words
- engage in a creative activity that allows for freedom of expression

CONTENT AND SKILLS

One of the most important functions of the sijo is to creatively express thoughts. Korean sijo is a hidden gem; it is easy to read and write and can provide historical information about Korean society and its people. Throughout this lesson, students will learn the cultural and political implications of sijo.

Writing sijo makes learning about Korean society more meaningful as students connect history to the present. Students analyze historic sijo and create their own poems, exploring and comparing historical social concerns to present day. Sijo does not need to be heavy; in fact, some of the best sijo are those with clever twists. Students can and will surprise themselves through creative expression.

BACKGROUND

The historic development of sijo is uncertain, although some sijo-like poems were written as early as the sixth century B.C. Originally, sijo were often sung by artisans who were accompanied by instrumentalists playing the flute and drum. As a result, sijo is lyrical in its approach. Early sijo were often about the beauty of nature, but sijo themes are quite broad. From the metaphysical to the profound, or even witty to personal, sijo themes vary widely. Unfortunately, many of the early sijo were not documented. This changed in the fifteenth century under the acclaimed King Sejong the Great due to his remarkable policies. In 1443, King Sejong commissioned Confucian scholars to create a Korean alphabet (*hangul*) specific to the Korean spoken language. Subsequently, more sijo were recorded, and the poetic form grew in popularity.

While not as commonly known as its Japanese counterpart haiku, sijo can easily be taught as it is flexible in its rules, format, and themes. Sijo is accessible for students as the potential for themes and content is broad and can be personal.

PROCEDURE

1. Read several modern sijo from Linda Sue Park's *Tap Dancing on the Roof.* Choose four or five poems to read to the students, or alternatively, project sijo on the board and have students read aloud. This introduces modern sijo in a fun, engaging manner.

2. Using Lucy Park's PowerPoint presentation (edits by Deb Holland), teach the basic information of sijo including history, format, and examples, both historic and modern. The PowerPoint includes sijo from D'Evelyn High School winners as this is my high school; feel free to add or adjust sijo. Play a *sijo chang* from the Sejong Cultural Society YouTube Channel.

3. Read and discuss the historic sijo in the PowerPoint for their historic references and connect them to current events or modern themes. Pay particular attention to Hwang Chini's sijo: read out of context, the sijo is about nature; read with an historical lens, it references society, relationships, and human emotion. In an historical context, the sijo is surprisingly complex, and students will appreciate the twist when they learn the sijo is about people.

4. After teaching the history of sijo and reviewing the historical examples, explain how to write a sijo. Highlight the format of sijo, with either three or six lines, and the surprise twist found in the last line. Explain the importance of the syllabic count and pattern in each line.

5. Students brainstorm ideas for their own sijo; this takes about ten to fifteen minutes.

6. Students complete and refine their sijo independently. This can be done the next day in class or for homework. Students can share their sijo with others.

ASSESSMENT

1. Students write a sijo for assessment. Evaluation can be based on completion, syllable count, its uniqueness, or even the cleverness of the twist. Encourage students to treat the assignment as if they were going to submit their sijo to the competition.

2. If a student wants to enter the sijo competition through the Sejong Cultural Society, take a closer look at the syllable count, cadence, and flow.

Works Cited

Holland, Deborah and Lucy Park. *Holland: Teaching Sijo.* Google Slide
 Presentation. Denver, Colorado, 2020.
 https://bit.ly/3AnYw8g

Kim, Wol-ha. Sijo chang.
 https://bit.ly/37qvkkD

Park, Linda Sue. *Tap Dancing on the Roof.* New York, Houghton Mifflin
 Company, 2007.
Park, Lucy. *Sijo: Korean Poetry, Structure and Samples.* PowerPoint
 Presentation. https://bit.ly/3Ao4WUS

Sejong Cultural Society website Resource page
 https://www.sejongculturalsociety.org/resources/

Reading and Writing Sijo

Tracy Kaminer

High School World Literature Teacher
Marist School, Atlanta, Georgia

INTRODUCTION

What follows is a suggested guideline for teaching sijo in a language arts classroom. The approach is for students in grades nine through twelve, but can be modified for seventh and eighth grade students. The material is intended to provide three days of teaching about sijo in fifty-five minute classes.

Day one could be the background material plus information on the Korean Wave and Korean history.

Day two could be the introduction to sijo, concluding with writing sijo.

Day three could be the sharing of the sijo created for homework.

The teaching objectives are to
- introduce Korean culture through a form of poetry particular to Korea
- read and understand important sijo in their cultural context

- understand and practice writing sijo

Materials used for this lesson plan come from
- *Early Korean Literature* by David McCann
- *The Bamboo Grove: An introduction to Sijo* by Richard Rutt
- "The Sijo, a Window into Korean Culture," from *Education About Asia* (Spring 2010) published by the Association for Asian Studies.

CREATING INTEREST

Before introducing students to a fourteenth century form of poetry written in Korea, introduce them to an aspect of Korean popular culture. If you have the means, show the "Dynamite" music video by Korean boy band BTS. You can find the video on YouTube. Another popular K-pop group is BLACKPINK. Their videos are also on YouTube. Why is this relevant? Students may be interested in knowing about the Korean Wave, which refers to the successful exporting of Korean culture since the 1990s. The impact of Korean culture, particularly in Asia, stems in part from the exporting of Korean soap operas and films.

QUICK LOOK AT KOREAN HISTORY

Hand out a chronology of Korean history. It is important for students to recognize the history of Korea. While students may be familiar with a few of the dates in modern history, such as those pertaining to the Korean War or Japanese occupation, they may know nothing about the famous Silla (Shilla) dynasty, known for artistic and cultural development, or the Joseon (Choson) dynasty under King Sejong. Point out that King Sejong was known as an inventor and among his achievements was the creation of the Korean alphabet, *hangul*.

The development of the Korean alphabet and language were important for Koreans whose formal communication and written history had been conducted in Chinese. According to Professor David McCann, even though Chinese continued to be the dominant form of written communication in Korea until the nineteenth century, "an opposing Korean character and spirit kept trying to assert itself," because of the development of *hangul*.

Important to the development of poetry in Korea was the state examination system. As in China, all educated men were trained in literature and composition as they prepared for the examinations that could qualify them for public service positions. From the fourteenth century on, the poems written by the scholars were either *kasa*, poems composed of an indefinite number of verses, or sijo.

TEACHING SIJO

A sijo is a three-line poem particular to Korea, developed in the fourteenth century. The poem introduces a theme in the first line, develops it in the second, has a twist or countertheme at the beginning of the third line, and concludes with a return to the original theme. The form of the poem relies on set phrasing and syllable count. Sijo were originally composed to be sung. Now they are literary works instead of musical ones.

Example 1:
by Chung Cheol (1536-1593)

A shadow strikes the water below; a monk passes by on the bridge,
"Stay awhile, reverend sir, let me ask you where you go."
He just points his staff at the white clouds and keeps on his way without turning.

Suggested Questions

- What is happening in the poem? (Literally, a monk is walking on a bridge, casting a shadow in the water. A person asks him where he is going. He points to the clouds and walks ahead.)
- Which words feel particularly important in the poem? (Some students may answer shadow; bridge; stay; go; points; clouds; keeps. Ask them what feels important about those words.)
- What do you think the theme of the poem is? (Some may talk about life as a journey; the difference between earth—shadow—and the Heavens—white cloud; the commitment of the monk and his focus on his goal.)
- What is the importance of the phrase that starts the third line, "He just points"? (Despite a speaker's attempt to get him to stay, the monk is focused on his journey; he doesn't even take the time to speak—he just points; his answer causes us to examine the difference in earth and sky, in the now and the hereafter.)
- Try to explain the poem in terms of theme, countertheme, and a return to the theme, the pattern of a sijo. (On a monk's life journey, he is asked to pause, to turn away from his goals; he points ahead, never turning away from his life's journey.)

Example 2
by Hwang Chini (sixteenth century)

Jade Green Stream, don't boast so proud of your easy passing through these blue hills.
Once you have reached the broad sea, to return again will be hard.
While the Bright Moon fills these empty hills, why not pause? Then go on, if you will.

- The same five questions. Students may respond that the theme is a kind of "seize the day" one about enjoying the moment. They may see it as a poem about nature and the inevitable flow of time.

- Ask the students to imagine that one character's name is Jade Green Stream and one character's name is Bright Moon. How would they then explain the story of the poem?

- Explain that this poem in the original language is divided into Chinese and Korean halves. The Chinese half of each line includes the words "Jade Green Stream in the blue hills; arriving at the broad sea; the Bright Moon filling the empty hills." The Korean second half of the poem includes the words "Don't boast; it is hard to return; pause and go." What do you notice about what the Korean language includes as opposed to what the Chinese language includes? What do you think is the point that the author is making? (According to Professor McCann, the Chinese half of the poem names and situates elements of the natural world; the Korean half un-names and dis-locates.)

- Share the story of the poem: Hwang Chini, the assumed author of the poem, was a *kisaeng*, a female entertainer, rather like a geisha in Japan. It was said that no man could resist her. She went by the name Bright Moon. A Confucian scholar-official, whose title was a homophone for Jade Green Stream, bragged that he could resist her and could pass through her region without stopping. She made up the song and when he heard it, he supposedly fell off his mule. According to Professor McCann, "The story frame makes the natural scenery a pun for the two humans, the man and woman, the official and the *kisaeng,* the two opposite poles of traditional Korean society. As happens over and over again in Korean folk literature, the cleverness of the vernacular makes the official, stuffy male seem a fool and topples him from his lofty yet precarious perch."

- On sijopoetry.com, you can listen to Professor McCann discuss this poem and perform part of it in Korean.
- Challenge: write a bilingual three-line poem. Write half of each line in English and half in a second language you know. Or write half of the line in standard English and half in another English dialect. Try to create a push and pull or tension in the use of the two languages. Share your experiments.

STRUCTURE OF A SIJO

Sijo poems are based on phrases with a certain number of syllables. Professor McCann explains that the lines of a sijo should feel as if they are unfolding, phrase by phrase. The first two lines are often similar or even identical in their phrasing and syllable counts. The third line has the all-important twist, which is always at the beginning of the third line and is always three syllables.

Standard Syllable Count

line	phrase one syllable count	phrase two syllable count	phrase three syllable count	phrase four syllable count
1	3	4	4 or 3	4
2	3	4	4 or 3	4
3	3	5	4	3

Important note on the last line: in many classic sijo, the first three syllables are often an exclamation or a word of strong emotional value. The phrase following that three syllable twist is normally the longest in the poem and gives a sense that the poem is about to conclude. By the end of the third line, the poem has come to an unsurprising ending. In sung sijo, the last phrase is often omitted altogether.

Sijo Written in English

Read the following Sejong Cultural Society sijo contest winners' poems. Identify the qualities that make each poem a winner. Stress theme, countertheme, and return to theme.

Untitled
by Creasy Clauser (twelfth grade, Crawfordsville, Indiana)

A single sole was lost today, deep in the river Yalu,
Thrashing, twisting, torn to shreds with color quickly fading.
On the bridge a small boy laughs, holding out his empty shoe.

Secret Song
by Taylor Edward (tenth grade, Euless, Texas)

You ask me what I'm humming; I tell you I'm humming about nothing.
This is untrue because I'm humming about you, all day long.
Who am I to tell you you're "nothing" when you are my song?

Cuisine?
by Jacob Diamond (eleventh grade, Weston, Florida)

I look through the window of the Korean barbeque place.
Ducks, chickens, creatures big and small, hang from the gallows of the cook.
Step inside and join the culture, leave your wishes at the door.

Activity one: Write a ten-minute sijo and share it

With the syllable and phrasing chart handy, write a quick sijo. It can be about anything—for instance, something that happened that day at school or at home. Work for the unfolding quality—phrase upon phrase with a three syllable twist in line three. The twist can be an exclamation or a question.

Activity two: Make a list of unlikely sijo topics

On the board create a student generated list of topics that you would not expect to be associated with sijo. They may include subjects such as neckties, pollen, bran muffins, and freezers. The list is intended to get students away from only focusing on broad topics such as summer and graduation.

Assignment

Ask students to write three sijo for homework. They should be proofed, edited, and typed. In class, they should choose one of the three to read aloud.

Activity three: Peer edit and advise

Ask students to trade sijo, concentrating on the ones read in class. Students should

- mark the phrases and count the syllables in each phrase in each other's sijo
- discuss their findings with the writer

- discuss whether the poem follows the sijo pattern
- discuss which phrases in the poem seem particularly effective and why
- mention difficulties in understanding and suggestions for improvement
- explain variations from the pattern

ASSIGNMENT

Students revise their sijo for homework and turn them in, edited and typed for a grade.

EXTENSION ASSIGNMENT

Have students teach sijo to someone else—a family member, a friend, a faculty member, or someone in the community. Ask students to write a one or two page process essay in which they discuss the steps they took to teach sijo, making mention of the difficulties and successes they had. They should write about what they learned in the process. They should then include a sijo from their "student."

Writing Haiku and Sijo:
Two East Asian Poetry Forms

Chuck Newell

High School English Teacher
Notre Dame High School, Chattanooga, Tennessee

Most students have written haiku in school. The three-line, seventeen-syllable Japanese poetic form is a staple of language arts curricula from about fourth grade on. These short poems are a good writing exercise and an introduction to Japanese culture. However, there is another type of East Asian poetry called a sijo (pronounced SHEE-jo) that is longer, with three lines and forty-five syllables that can challenge students. The sijo can also be a good tool for introducing students to Korean culture.

Japan has been a familiar East Asian culture in America since World War II. We probably all have some knowledge about their society, their exports, their movies, and, of course, their poetry. However, for the past few decades, we have become stronger trading partners with Korea and more Korean immigrants and students have been coming to America, bringing their unique culture with them. Teaching students how to write sijo and how it is different from haiku is a good first step in studying East Asia. Learning about sijo can also help Korean and Korean/American students connect with their own culture.

Haiku has become popular because it can be easy to write.

Students do not have to worry about rhyme; they simply must compose a three line poem that describes a certain event or image and have five syllables in the first line, seven in the second, and five in the third. However, there are more subtle rules to composing haiku. They should be in the present tense, focus on nature or a season, and create a single image in the reader's mind. Thus, such poems remind us of elements important to Japanese culture: nature, beauty, and impermanence.

A good example would be this classic poem from the haiku master Basho (please note that translations of haiku from Japanese into English often do not have a perfect five-seven-five form):

Coolness of the melons
flecked with mud
in the morning dew

This poem creates a single image of nature in the mind of the reader and is a good example of how to write haiku.

There are many books and web sites that have great classic and modern examples of haiku and instructions on how to write them. The case is not the same for sijo. This poetic form has been around for at least seven hundred years, but not much is known about it in America. Sijo are often about nature, though they do not have to be. Like haiku, sijo have a three-line structure, but the form is more complicated and thus the meaning more complex. Sijo should have around forty-five syllables (its syllable count is not as strict as haiku) and thus each line should have about fifteen syllables. In addition, each line has a function. The first line introduces the theme, the second line develops or expands the theme, and the third line begins with an ironic twist or surprise, and then the last part of the third line concludes the poem. This irony or surprise at the end of the poem is what separates the sijo from the haiku.

Here is an example of a twentieth-century sijo from the Korean poet Yi Ho-u:

Rain

I hear the rain beating, breathlessly on the banana leaves.
All plants begin to sprout, craving nature's grace.
Worried about his farmwork, an old man opens his door and listens.

This poem clearly has a nature-based theme like a haiku, but with more syllables and with the inclusion of irony, it adds depth to the image. Also, most classic sijo have a pause in the middle of each line; this adds to the musical quality in the original Korean since the poems were first written to be sung.

ACTIVITY

To show the difference between these two poetic forms, have students write a haiku about an image or incident. Then, have them write a sijo about the same topic. They will have to add detail and complexity to their sijo.

For example, have students write a haiku about an outdoor activity they enjoy. Require them to use a season to help create a moment in time. (Note that using a title can give meaning and focus to the image they create):

Spring Mountain Biking

Pedaling through trees
Odor of honeysuckle
Flash of wildflowers

Then, using the same title, have students turn the situation into a sijo, making sure to include an ironic turn at the end. Ask students to include more images and details to expand the syllable count to about fifteen per line. When writing their first sijo, I tell students just to make sure they have fourteen to sixteen syllables per line. The more complex use of syllables can wait for future lessons.

Spring Mountain Biking

Pedaling through the forest, dappled sun on the handle bars
The sweet smell of honeysuckle and the flash of wildflowers
Almost makes one forget your straining lungs, your burning muscles

Note that the final line of this sijo is a new invention. It is a comment on the basic imagery of the haiku. This is a good technique to add the twist or irony at the end.

LESSON EXTENSIONS

Give students examples of classical Chinese poetry by Li Bai and Du Fu to see if they notice differences in their subject matter and attitudes.

Works Cited

Higginson, William and Penny Harter. *The Haiku Handbook: How to Write, Share, and Teach Haiku.* Tokyo, Kodansha International, 1985.

Kim, Jaihiun. *Modern Korean Verse in Sijo Form. Selected and Translated by Jaihium Kim.* Vancouver, BC, Ronsdale Press, 1997.

Sijo Teaching Guide for Children

Seo Kwan-ho

A sijo poet, educator, and publisher of *Children's Sijo World*
translated and adapted by Lucy Park

INTRODUCTION

This guide is for teachers who intend to teach a three-day sijo lesson to children. I have used this guide for sijo instruction at many schools. Most children who attended were able to write sijo after six hours of lessons. I recommend a few tips for teachers.

First, encourage students to write something they personally experienced. It is difficult to write sijo on topics they have not experienced. Children have plenty of things to talk about: birthdays, mothers, playgrounds, schools, friends, or school festivals. It will be easy for them to write on these topics.

Second, ask students to read and memorize as many sijo as they can. It will become part of their thinking process. Then when they try to write sijo, they will be able to write one effortlessly. Please visit the Sejong Cultural Society website resource page for sijo samples. More award-winning sijo can be found on the website writing competition page under past winners.

Third, require students to write a diary in sijo at least one day a week. While writing events or feelings, sijo will become part of their life.

Fourth, ask students to write sijo on one small fact, event, or feeling that stirred up deep emotion. Writing about several things or long stories will create a narrative, but not a good sijo. The student must focus on one thing that will touch readers deep in their hearts.

Fifth, have students write a sijo with a single theme over three lines. Remind them the sijo must have a theme that runs through all lines.

Characteristics of Poetry

- Poems express thoughts and feelings. Writing only facts will not make poems.
- Poems are short and have condensed messages.
- Poems use symbols, metaphor, allusion, simile, inference, etc.
- Poets must have a beautiful mind to write beautiful poems.
- A poem must have a unique story and a theme.
- Poets write poems to induce empathy from readers.
- Poems are stories.
- Poets can write good poems when they read, memorize, and recite well-written poems of others.

CHARACTERISTICS OF SIJO

- Sijo is a unique poetry form from Korea.
- Sijo is a song that expresses and describes events of the past or events of our time.
- Sijo includes only essential words, without modifiers, decorative words, or descriptive explanation.
- Sijo-writers often avoid conjunctions or conjunctive adverbs.
- Sijo must have a conclusion in the third line.
- Sijo is written in a fixed format like food arranged nicely on a pretty plate.
- Sijo includes three lines, six phrases, and twelve segments.
- Sijo must include unique content to persuade or to induce empathy from readers.
- Sijo must have a musical quality.
- Sijo can be sung naturally because of its syllabic structure.

STRUCTURE OF SIJO

When writing sijo, the poet introduces a theme or idea in the first line, develops the theme to the next level in the second line, and brings it to a big strike or a twist in the third line. The third line is the climax, with a dramatic reversal or twist. The first half of the third line comprises two segments of three and five syllables, which will be the climax. The second half of the third line is written in four and three syllables to bring it to a safe ending and render a sense of closure. The goal is to evoke excitement and bring closure.

A sijo includes two components: clearly stated story and musical quality. In a well written sijo, the theme or story must be stated to be persuasive to the readers. The musical quality is achieved by using the proper syllable counts. Reciting a sijo with musical quality often makes one feel as though one is singing a beautiful song.

The basic structure uses the following syllable counts in 3 lines; 15 syllables in each line, 45 syllables in total. Slight variation may occur but the beginning of the third line must start with 3 syllables. The first part of the third line (3-5) is used to introduce a surprise turn or twist or climax, followed by a resolution of the climax or conclusion in the next part (4-3).

3-4-4-4   (15 total)
3-4-4-4   (15 total)
3-5-4-3   (15 total)

SUGGESTED TOPICS FOR SIJO

Topics for sijo can come from anything in everyday life. Consider the following examples:
- Personal or public events
- People
- Food, fruits, vegetables
- What you do naturally
- Humor
- School or office
- School or office supplies
- Toys
- Exercise
- Outings with family or friends
- Flowers, plants, trees
- Animals, livestock, zoo
- Earth, nature, season changes, weather
- Virtue
- Events or activities related to finance

- Travel, scenic spots
- Imaginary world, spiritual world, dreams

WRITING PHRASES AND LINES

Write phrases and lines with 3-4 syllables, 4-4 syllables, 3-5 syllables, or 4-3 syllables. The following examples are phrases of award-winning sijo from the Sejong Writing Competition:

Syllable counts	Phrases and lines that expand to the next phrase	Concluding phrase and line
3-4	That sweater, so warm and soft	My new dog, little Emma
3-4	My aunt passed, stupid cancer	On the moon, I plant our flag
4-4	Tough decisions. "No one wears it."	I'm heading home, straight to my bed
4-4	You have become your own leader	Tiny snow-white egret wading
3-5	As I fade from your memory	I look down, my collar is gone
3-5	Ordered by a relentless wind	You became your own enemy
4-3	The dark abyss swells below	A gift to us from his friend
4-3	A universe made of stars	She is still here, on four paws

Writing Sijo

I recommend students write sijo without conjunctions or conjunctive adverbs (e.g. and, therefore, then).

Example 1
Theme: gratitude, blessings, gift

Birthday Present

I scored more than ten goals today, with these running shoes, mom's present
(received birthday present), (and then)
Birthday candles still burning in my heart, every day is my birthday
(happy feeling) (and therefore)
Mom, with these shoes, I will score more than hundreds of goals
(I want to pay back)

열 골도 더 넣었다, 어머니 운동화로
(받음) (그래서)
날마다 생일 같다, 촛불이 타고 있다
(느낌) (그러니까)
어머니 이 운동화로 백 골도 더 넣을게요
(보답)

Example 2
Theme: love, happiness

Little Brother

At the dawn of that morning, my little brother was born
(birth of my brother, fact)
Yesterday was his second birthday, he brought joy to our family
(my thoughts, meaning or significance, my feeling)
Our family, so full of love, you and I are brothers
(conclusion)

동트는 이른 아침 동생이 태어났다
(탄생 - 사실)
어제가 두 돌인데 집안의 기쁨이다
(의미 - 생각)
온 가족 넘치는 사랑, 너와 나는 한 형제
(결론 - 떨침)

Sijo Format Variations

A. Gradual Progression (A→A1→A2)

Spread out the poet's idea as the event unfolds based on time, place, circumstance, or action.

Drinking Spring Rain '봄비 먹으면'
by Yoo Young-Ae, 유영애
translated by Lucy Park

When grass seeds drink spring rain,
    new sprouts and blades spring out.
When flower seeds drink spring rain,
    flowers bloom and fragrance emerges.
When my heart drinks spring rain,
    a poet inside of me is awakened.

풀씨가 봄비 먹으면 눈트고 새잎나고
꽃씨가 봄비 먹으면 꽃피고 향기나고
가슴이 봄비 먹으면 시인이 눈을뜨고

B. Following in sequence (A→B→C)

Three different lines, one connecting to the next.
- Observation of daily life: introduce theme, expand theme, conclusion.
- Compare to hiking: start at the bottom of a hill, climb, arrive at the peak.

B.1. LINEAR THOUGHTS (A→B→C)

Balsam Flowers (first verse) '봉숭아' 첫수
by Kim Sang-ok, 김상옥
translated by Lucy Park

After rain, in the backyard,
　　the balsam flowers opened halfway.
Alone, I watch these flowers
　　blooming year after year.
Why not write about them in detail
　　and send it to my sister?

비 오자 장독간에 봉숭아 반만 벌어
해마다 피는 꽃을 나만 두고 볼 것인가
세세한 사연을 적어 누님께로 보내자.

B.2. LINEAR PROCESS (A→B→C)

Spring Thoughts (first verse) '봄 생각' 첫수
by Chung Wan-young, 정완영
translated by Lucy Park

Spring rain came last night,
　　drizzling all night—pitter patter.
This morning, many tiny green leaves
　　sprouted in our vegetable patch.
When will these tiny leaves
　　grow as big as butterfly wings?

어젯밤 도란도란 상추비가 내리더니
오늘 아침 텃밭에는 파란 싹이 돋아났네
언제쯤 예쁜 속잎이 나비만큼 자랄까.

B.3. LINEAR ACTION (A→B→C)

Baby and Flower Bed '아기와 꽃밭'
by Seo Kwan-ho, 서관호
translated by Lucy Park

A baby is toddling into the flower bed, wobbling, wobbling.
The curious sun follows the baby with a big, bright grin.
When the baby looks up, a peony opens into full bloom.

아기가 꽃밭으로 아장아장 걸어가요
해님이 신기한지 방긋방긋 따라와요
아기가 고개를 들면 함박꽃이 화알짝.

C. TIE TOGETHER (A→A1=C)

Put two facts or actions together and make one set, as if you put one sock and another sock together to make a pair.

Boonie's Apricot Tree '분이네 살구나무'
by Chung Wan-young, 정완영
translated by Lucy Park

The smallest house in our village—
    Boonie's little shanty house.
The tallest tree in our village—
    Boonie's apricot tree.
Bursting into full bloom overnight,
    it looms larger than a king's palace.

*Boonie is the name of a little girl.

동네서 젤 작은 집 분이네 오막살이
동네서 젤 큰 나무 분이네 살구나무

밤사이 활짝 펴올라 대궐보다 덩그렇다

D. Conclusion first, explanation later (C=A+B)

State your conclusion first, and then explain the theme in the next two lines: why that is or why it happened that way.

Composing Music '작곡 중'
by Seo Kwan-ho, 서관호
from *Short Sunflower* 2011, an anthology of sijo for children
translated by Lucy Park

Sparrows are sitting on power lines
    composing new music.
Tiny bodies are music notes—
    measure after measure,
busily chirping, tweeting,
    fine-tuning the new melody.

제비들이 전깃줄에 작곡을 하고 있다
마디마디 모닥모닥 음표를 그려놓고
음정을 조율하느라 지지배배 바쁘다.

E. Sudden twist or turn (A→T→B) on the second or third lines

Twist or big turn at the second or third line. Do not use "but" or similar connecting words.

Light bulb '전등'
by Seo Kwan-ho, 서관호
translated by Lucy Park

Studying into late night, keep dozing off, *kkambak kkambak**
The light bulb does not doze off, becomes brighter and brighter
Thank you light bulb! I, too, want to be the light of the world

밤늦게 공부하다 졸려서 깜박깜박
전등은 졸지 않고 더 밝게 힘을 낸다
전등아! 정말 고마워, 나도 세상 비출게

* *Kkambak kkambak* is a Korean onomatopoeia describing a person
  dozing off and falling into sleep for split seconds repeatedly, as if
  light bulbs are flickering.

Writing Sijo Using Chain of Thoughts

Example 1. Dragonfly

Experience	A dragonfly flies around.
Your thoughts or feelings on this experience	Summer is here already.
Following thoughts	1. It flies around like a jet plane performing stunts. 2. It is fun to watch the dragonfly.
Next step of following thoughts	1. I want to show it to my brother. 2. This will make a good toy for him.
Final sijo	**Dragonfly** A dragonfly flies around; it must be summer already. Watching it is such fun, like a jet plane performing stunts. I want to show it to my brother, it will make a good toy for him.

Example 2. Scarecrow

Experience	A scarecrow is standing alone in an empty field after the harvest.
Your thoughts or feelings on this experience	1. It must be cold and lonely. 2. What is it thinking?
Following thoughts	1. It must be very cold at night. 2. How awful does it feel standing here alone at night? 3. They made it work hard and abandoned it after the harvest. 4. Why did they not take it to their home?
Next step of following thoughts	My grandmother is living in the countryside. She must feel lonely and cold, just like that scarecrow.
Final sijo	**Scarecrow** The empty field after harvest, a scarecrow is standing alone. What's it thinking? The chilly autumn wind is blowing. My grandma is in the countryside; is the chilly wind blowing there, too?

Sijo Writing Worksheet (1)

*Worksheet based on Sijo Teaching Guide by Seo Kwan-ho

Experience	
Your thoughts or feelings on this experience	
Following thoughts	
Next step of following thoughts	
Final sijo 3-4-4(3)-4 3-4-4(3)-4 3-5-4-3	

Sijo Writing Worksheet (2)

*Worksheet based on Sijo Teaching Guide by Seo Kwan-ho

First Line				
syllable count	3	4	4 (3)	4
Introduce your story or theme				
Second Line				
syllable count	3	4	4 (3)	4
Expand your theme or go deeper into your story				
Third Line				
syllable count	**3***	5	4	3
End with 'twist', something surprising or unexpected				

*Always try to start the first segment of the third line with 3 syllables
Example: *Still American* by Roberto Santos (first place winner, 2013 Sejong Writing Competition)

	First segment	Second segment	Third segment	Fourth segment
(syllable count) First Line	3	4	4	4
	They say go,	return to land	that I don't know.	It makes no sense.
(syllable count) Second Line	3	4	4	4
	Born and raised	American,	so Mexico	is still foreign.
(syllable count) Third Line	**3**	5	4	3
	Culture kept,	but this is my home.	Immigrant, no:	Hispanic.

Download worksheets from https://bit.ly/3iN94bb

Sijo Writing Worksheet (3)

*Modified from Sijo's Three Lines by Liz Jorgensen

	Syllable count		My sijo
First line: Introduce your story. Think about what your characters are doing and where they are.	3		
	4		
	4		
	4		
Second lin: Go deeper into your story. Think about what is happening and why you're telling this story.	3		
	4		
	4		
	4		
Third line: Include a twist. Think about something that is unexpected or surprising or a change.	3		
	5		
	4		
	3		

Download worksheets from https://bit.ly/3iN94bb

PART III

My Favorite Sijo

drawings by Wonsook Kim

This chapter features commentary on prize-winning sijo from the Sejong Cultural Society's annual competition since 2008. Sijo experts, scholars, teachers, and authors select their favorite winning sijo and provide an explanation why the poem is their favorite.

Sijo in this chapter are listed in chronological order, using the year the poem was chosen. After each poem is the poet's bio; the bio often includes information on the sijo's inspiration. Following the bio is the sijo enthusiast's commentary.

Dreams on a Lake

by Michael Chung, third place 2008

I'm floating on the dark lake, dreaming I'm floating on a cloud
The surface of my tanned skin tingling as water dries on it
A man yells, "Hello, good neighbor!" breaking my dreams to pieces.

MICHAEL CHUNG, FIFTH GRADE, LOS ANGELES, CALIFORNIA

I found out about this contest last year when my older brother, Richard, brought home a flyer from his school. Although I had never heard of a sijo before the competition, I enjoyed this type of writing. Somehow, it seemed easy to express my feelings in this format. Later, I found out from my mom that our family starter, on my dad's side, sixteen generations ago, Chung Cheol, was considered the best sijo writer in all of Korea at the time. He wrote "Samiinkok," a poem known by all Koreans.

My hobbies are playing piano, building complex Legos, and technology. I want to be an entrepreneur, but I am still not sure in what field. Some days I want to make computers; some days I want to build cars; some days I want to start a company like Samsung, which makes refrigerators, cars, computers, and other electronics.

My personal hero is Admiral Yi Sun-sin, who protected Korea (then known as Joseon) from Japanese invaders from 1592-1598. In the last battle, when Japan retreated, Yi Sun-sin was hit in his heart by a stray bullet. However, he acted as if he was not harmed in order to not distract his soldiers. When Korea finally triumphed, he died. I admire that he defeated the Japanese navy of three hundred ships, even though he had only twelve ships. I also admire that he fought to stay alive to see his soldiers victorious.

DAVID MCCANN, PROFESSOR EMERITUS OF KOREAN LITERATURE, HARVARD UNIVERSITY, AND A POET

I have enjoyed so much the way the sijo has been able to move into English language practice. "Dreams on a Lake" is one of three sijo poems that are my real favorites and goes back to the very beginning of the contest.

"Dreams on a Lake" works so well as a sijo poem, starting things moving in the first line, as the I floats, dreaming, into the second line, which continues the narrative, adding detail. A big loud twist at the beginning of line three, as "A man yells," and then the perfect crumble of the conclusion as the poem ends. Marvelous!

Untitled

by Creasy Clauser, first place 2009

A single sole was lost today, deep in the river Yalu,

Thrashing, twisting, torn to shreds with color quickly fading.

On the bridge a small boy laughs, holding out his empty shoe.

CREASY CLAUSER, TWELFTH GRADE, CRAWFORDSVILLE, INDIANA

In poetry class the last trimester of my senior year, my teacher started a unit on cultural poetry. One of our assignment choices was to write a sijo. After I spent what seemed like forever thinking about writing it, I decided to go with a humorous approach. Upon turning my sijo in, my teacher recommended that I let her submit it into this contest for me.

Writing the sijo turned out to be a lot of fun. Getting the correct syllable count was really hard, but after a lot of trial and error, I figured out how to manipulate and rearrange the words to still say everything I wanted and convey the same story. As it is with all poetry it seems, some sacrifices had to be made, but the resulting product was better than I had ever imagined it would be.

As for my future plans, next year I will be attending Rose-Hulman Institute of Technology to major in biomedical engineering as well as run track, cross country, and participate in the band and music programs. My hobbies and interests include photography, reading, playing sports, and anything to do with band. I play clarinet, piano, flute, and pit percussion. I am also a member of New Hope Christian Church.

My personal heroes are my parents. They have taught me so much, and been supportive of every activity I have wanted to try. I couldn't be where I am now without them.

DAVID MCCANN, PROFESSOR EMERITUS OF KOREAN LITERATURE, HARVARD UNIVERSITY, AND A POET

I couldn't get over the fun, the play with the language in "A single sole was lost today." But it was a fish! Not a soul. And then on the bridge, the little boy whose shoe lost its sole. And the boy, the small boy who laughs and holds out an empty shoe, which we might guess is the poem. What fun!

Secret Song

by Taylor Edwards, second place 2009

You ask me what I'm humming; I tell you I'm humming about nothing.

This is untrue because I'm humming about you, all day long.

Who am I to tell you you're "nothing" when you are my song?

TAYLOR EDWARDS, TENTH GRADE, EULESS, TEXAS

I'm sixteen years old and about to be a junior at Trinity

High School in Euless, Texas. YAY! GO TROJANS! I entered the writing competition because my AP/IB English teacher, Mrs. Nease, suggested that I should after grading my sijo assignment. Honestly I didn't have the faintest expectation of winning anything; I just did it for the fun of it all.

What I learned through writing this sijo, is that when I write anything, I can never come up with something *good* without a *great* inspiration.

My goal in the future is to be a marine biologist or an orthodontist...but more on the marine biologist side because it sounds like a lot of fun. I don't want to aim for a career just because I would make a lot of money for doing it, I want to look forward to going to work, and not have to drag my feet to get there. So I'm pretty much open to anything.

Some of my hobbies and personal interests are being on the gymnastics team at school, running alone at the crack of dawn, lifeguarding in the summer at the city pool, rock climbing with friends, taking nature pictures, going camping with my family, kayaking on Grapevine Lake, and my favorite thing ever is going to the beach in North Carolina. Oh, and lime-green is the best color in the history of forever.

I don't really have a personal hero, but in general I do admire people with strong opinions that don't give in to the influence of others, no matter how tempting the bad influence might be.

DAVID MCCANN, PROFESSOR EMERITUS OF KOREAN LITERATURE, HARVARD UNIVERSITY, AND A POET

"Secret Song" by Taylor Edwards struck me as a poem about a poem. It's not the poet speaking, but the poem itself, turning itself inside-out to make the poignant comment about what a poem really is, "nothing." Which is everything!

Sijo Sijo

by Alex Griffin, second place 2011

As I write this Sijo

      Not a thought comes in my mind

Topics escaped, I am lost

      What shall I write? I don't know.

The seasons? Maybe small bears?

      Won't ever know. Sijo is done.

ALEX GRIFFIN, ELEVENTH GRADE, OCONOMOWOC, WISCONSIN

Alex Griffin attended Arrowhead Union High School in

Hartland, Wisconsin.

MOLLY GAUDRY, PH.D., POET, AUTHOR, AND EDUCATOR

In these spare lines, Alex Griffin offers a fun, surprising journey for the reader. The speaker of the poem begins by providing meta-commentary about being in the act of writing "this Sijo," and although the speaker says, "Not a thought comes," we understand this to mean, instead, that the *right* thought, the *best* poetic thought, does not come. And what writer can't relate to that? For the next two lines, the speaker continues to lament their further loss of potential poetic material. Then, in the fifth line, two possible topics come into view—"The seasons? Maybe small bears?" In this moment, although the poem (about an unwritten poem) is not about the seasons and is not about small bears, it gets to have its cake and eat it too: it becomes, in fact, a poem about the seasons, and a poem about small bears—it becomes a poem about all the things that a poem about the seasons, or a poem about small bears, *could* be. And then the wry speaker's voice returns: "Won't ever know. Sijo is done." Once again: highly relatable content for any writer. Ultimately, what I love about this poem is its awareness about all the things it *could* be about; and in this way, the small poem ends up representing so much more than what is here. For imaginative readers, this sijo's possibilities might be endless.

I Have Heard

by Hollister Rhone, first place 2012

I can speak the language of tigers, I can understand their words.

I can hear the honey bees, the bears, the lions, and the birds.

I can tell the mice what's on my mind, and I've heard. Yes, I have heard.

HOLLISTER RHONE, FIFTH GRADE, CHICAGO, ILLINOIS

I entered this competition after my English teacher, Mrs. Wallace (Ted Lenart Regional Gifted Center), announced this contest to my class and encouraged all of us to submit a poem.

This type of poetry was new to me so I gave it a shot. In fact, it was really fun! At first it was hard to think of an idea for the sijo poem, but then it hit me! My family had been fostering a pit bull terrier named Gomez. When we found him as a stray it was clear that he had been abused and neglected for most of his life. During his first few weeks with us he seemed really sad. It was then that I realized he had no voice when he was being abused on the streets. He couldn't do anything about it except run. I started thinking that maybe animals do have voices and you just have to listen carefully to hear them. That's why I wrote this poem.

My future goal is simple. To keep writing. Whenever I have an idea, I write it down, and I want to continue to do that. I am on a high-level competitive gymnastics team, and between writing and gymnastics, there's nothing more I can ask for.

EMILY YOON, AUTHOR OF A CRUELTY SPECIAL TO OUR SPECIES, POETRY EDITOR FOR THE MARGINS

The sijo "I Have Heard" is rife with playful mystery. The identity of the speaker that can speak the languages of beasts and insects is not revealed, but the repetition of "I can" lends a childlike air to the voice, which suggests that the conversations with the bees and animals are from a young, powerful imagination. However, another repetition appears in the third and final line: "I've [I have] heard." The sijo's last sentence also includes the assured "Yes." This affirmative and the surprising repetition bestow a godlike quality to the voice, transforming the speaker from a human child to an omni audient being, thereby introducing a "twist" that is fundamental to sijo.

At the end of the poem, the reader is left wondering: what has the "I" heard? Rhone could have easily inserted an object after the verb "heard" the first time it appears, but instead, only restates and affirms the act of hearing. The poet deliberately leaves the question unanswered, refusing to offer a clean closure —a clever choice that extends the sijo's "life" to continue beyond what has been said in the mere forty seven syllables. "I Have Heard" is an excellent example of a poem that expands its meanings and possibilities boundlessly within the confines of its formal rules; it is a poem that demonstrates that form is not a limiting tool.

Still American

by Roberto Santos, first place 2013

They say go, return to land that I don't know. It makes no sense.

Born and raised American, so Mexico is still foreign.

Culture kept, but this is my home. Immigrant, no: Hispanic.

ROBERTO SANTOS, TWELFTH GRADE, LAREDO, TEXAS

I had first heard of this competition as a class assignment for my English Four (John B. Alexander High School) class and winning first place came as a great surprise! Without my teacher pushing the class to join, I probably would've never done it out of fear of failure. The fact that I won something for just writing thoughts I've always had with a creative twist still blows my mind!

I live in a border town made up of a Hispanic/Mexican majority, where Spanish is spoken just as much as English; although I'm proud of my heritage, English is still my primary language. In my spare time I make music with my friends and spend time with my family. I plan on majoring in musical engineering to help expose some of my talented friends' music.

Thanks to this competition I have more confidence in my academic capabilities and feel inspired to participate in more writing competitions.

MARY CONNOR, AUTHOR, EDUCATOR, AND CO-FOUNDER, NATIONAL KOREAN STUDIES

Roberto Santos creates a sijo poem that is powerful, personal, and relevant. While he was born in America, he identifies himself as American and Hispanic. His poem speaks to his life and the experience of many children whose parents came to the United States for a better life. Roberto has been raised in two cultures and takes pride in both, but he recognizes that thousands of his contemporaries fear that they may have to return to a land that they do not know. He observes the recommended syllable count and his diction is effective.

ELGIN-BOKARI T. SMITH (A.K.A. L O KARI), TEACHER, MUSIC ARTIST, AND ELEPHANT REBELLION AMBASSADOR

The words of Roberto Santos. A sijo I know like the back of my hand. The Sejong Cultural Society gave Elephant Rebellion the honor of taking this fantastic sijo and transforming these words into the inspiration for our song "Still American". As a black man growing up in this country, I often feel like I must walk multiple paths and always explain my existence in spaces. "Go back to where you came from," is often said as if I was not born here, as if I didn't walk these streets paved by the blood and sweat of my ancestors. As if we have not been here. Roberto, grade twelve, already had a clear understanding of who he is and where he belongs, which is wherever his feet land. I also love how he said, "Culture kept," which, for me, indicates he comes from a family with values, creativity, and a sense of their identity. America is his home. America is our home, and he will continue to stand. Immigrant no, Hispanic. I felt his words were powerful and affirming.

Untitled

by Hapshiba Kwon, first place 2014

Rustling fabrics, I explore seas of tweed, paisley blouses, and plaid.

Tangible remembrances; your days of youth, have become mine.

Clothed in strength, now you chase no trends. Wrinkled, gray, lovely threads.

HAPSHIBA KWON, TENTH GRADE, CERRITOS, CALIFORNIA

I learned of this contest through my school (Whitney High School) and thoroughly struggled with creating such a short poem. However, writing the sijo really helped me notice the power and purpose that each word holds in meaningful works of literature.

I enjoy bike riding, writing, reading, drawing, and taking photos of things other than myself. My personal heroes include Jesus Christ, who I strive to be more like, and my parents. My parents have truly played a big role in my life and have supported me in doing all things.

I aspire to become an author. I dream of publishing a book that will be accessible to everyone, everywhere.

Lee Herrick, MFA, author, poet, and educator

I admire how this sijo is an entire world and story within the form's relative brevity. The economy of language, the precise images, and the fabric textures are impressive, too. I love the "seas of tweed, paisley blouses, and plaid." These styles place the person's clothes from a certain decade, in my mind, which is an admirable, deft touch of detail. In the second line, the speaker addresses someone: a family member, someone older, someone whose "tangible remembrances" have become the speaker's clothes now. The poet writes, "your days of youth, have become mine." Here we move beyond the gift or inheritance of clothes into the ways our lives often mirror the lives of our elders. The other person now "chase[s] no trends," which the speaker seems to admire. The poet's respect for the other person's "strength" is evident. The closing image, "Wrinkled, gray, lovely threads," is wonderful. It captures emotion, character, and physicality all at once. The "threads" open up the poem at the end and allow readers to imagine their own relationships with this poem and with the people in their own lives. I found myself thinking about my parents, their clothes, their youth. I think of my own life, my own fleeting youth, and my daughter's future. To go on a journey like this after reading this wonderful poem is to remember what poetry can do.

Ivanna Yi, assistant professor of Korea Studies, Cornell University

Hapshiba Kwon's untitled sijo centers on a meaningful intergenerational exchange that may have gone overlooked without this poem. The tactile experience of handling the clothes of an older family member opens a space for a young person to acknowledge both her physical and emotional maturity as she accepts the gift. The specificity of tweed, paisley, and plaid leads to a celebration of the older family member, who is now "Clothed in strength," chasing "no trends." Through their bond, this is a strength she also inherits.

Overcoming the Limitations

by Zion Kim, first place 2015

They laughed when he struggled in his wheelchair, begging to join them.

They laughed when they heard him speak an awkward string of gibberish.

They saw him stand from the chair with determined eyes. They did not laugh.

ZION KIM, ELEVENTH GRADE, LITTLE NECK, NEW YORK

Writing a sijo poem in English was, for me, like having one foot in one world and the other foot in a completely different world. I was immediately interested in this contest because although growing up in this country has led me to assimilate to the American culture, I have always been very proud of being Korean and jumped at any opportunity to embrace my heritage. The sijo allowed me to express both my American side as well as my Korean side, representing the beautiful balance between two opposites that both carry so much meaning in my life.

The story behind my sijo is also deeply rooted in my personal life. I have a brother with multiple disabilities, and growing up with him has created in me a deep understanding of how difficult life is for the disabled and a burning passion to work for them to one day gain the recognition and acceptance they deserve in our critical society. I wanted to express this compassion I have in my sijo, so I wrote about the moment when a man in a wheelchair decides not to let his disabilities limit him from reaching his potential or exclude him from the world.

I hope that through my sijo, people will be able to see, at least for a moment, life through the eyes of those who endure discrimination, misunderstanding, and all sorts of hardships because of their disabilities. I'm sincerely thankful that I had this chance to express parts of myself that I hold very dear to my heart.

JOONOK HUH, PROFESSOR EMERITUS, ENGLISH DEPARTMENT, UNIVERSITY OF NORTHERN COLORADO

The essence of short-form poetry is the quick realization, the inescapable vision, the enlightenment imparted to the reader in relatively few lines. In his poem "In a Station of the Metro" (1913), derived from Japanese haiku, American poet Ezra Pound gives us a breathtaking image of transience, comparing faces he sees at the underground Metro in Paris to "petals on a wet, black bough." In her "First Fight. Then Fiddle." (1949), African-American poet Gwendolyn Brooks effectively uses the Italian/Petrarchan Sonnet form for her message about race, art, and the use of power. By these two examples, we see poetry as historically located yet transcendent: the faces at the underground station are all our faces; the struggle with race is all our struggles.

Sijo is another example. Incepted at the end of the fourteenth century in Korea, during the last days of the Goryeo dynasty, sijo has become popularized in the western world, especially in America, during the second half of the twentieth century, as shown through the high interest for the annual Sejong Cultural Society Sijo Competition. In three short lines, the traditional Korean sijo presents a wide spectrum of human affairs from politics to romances and from natural beauty to social practices, in philosophical and meditative tones. Its language tends to be personal and lyrical, and employ images instead of direct expressions. The theme of sijo is introduced in the first line, developed in the second line, and then some twist, witty or powerful, is provided in the third line.

"Overcoming the Limitations" is a beautifully-constructed and powerfully-delivered sijo. In the traditional sijo form, it presents a personal effort to overcome one's limitations and yet the very story of the personal effort serves as a metaphor for the larger-scale limitations that we are facing in America and in the rest of the world: for instance, the hierarchic class structure, discrimination against under-represented groups, and the Black Lives Matter movement.

The identical beginning of the first and second lines of "Overcoming the Limitations" sets up the hierarchy between "them" and "him" right away. "They laughed" at his physical disability and at his unintelligible speech. The central image in the first line is the wheelchair and in the second line "a string of gibberish." He looks different and speaks differently from them, which makes him a laughing stock. In his poem "Persimmons," Indonesian-American poet Li-Young Lee portrays a boy slapped by Mrs. Walker, his teacher, for not being able to differentiate the pronunciation of persimmon and precision. "A string of gibberish" represents not only a physical condition but cultural, speech differences. Tensions build up from the very beginning of the sijo with "They laughed when..." and wait for the moment of explosion. And it does when he stands up in the third line— perhaps as culturally impactful as the explosion of deferred dreams in Langston Hughes' poem "Harlem." When he stands up, they do not laugh. The laughing ones become silent when the silenced one stands from the wheelchair and faces them.

What I see in Kim's three-line sijo is something universal, global. When life unfairly brings a person down, s/he needs to stand up. Kim's sijo is an excellent example of short-form poetry exploding enlightenment into consciousness, ever expanding the limits of our compassion.

Emma

by Austin Snell, first place 2016

My new dog, little Emma, a gift to us from the heavens.
My aunt passed, stupid cancer, my mom distraught. Everyone muted.
I could look into Emma's eyes, she's still here, on four paws.

AUSTIN SNELL, TWELFTH GRADE, HARTLAND, WISCONSIN

I enjoy playing sports, especially soccer. I don't play on the school's team, but I enjoy kicking and shooting the ball.

I am a fan of the London soccer team Arsenal F.C. I am a huge car enthusiast. I love motorsport (specifically Formula 1 and Rally) and I would love to race cars in the future. I plan on going to college to learn about automotive engineering because I like the technical nature and the precision of cars. I work well with my hands. I always thought of being a mechanic, since I am passionate about cars, but I don't really like grime and getting filthy.

I would love to thank my Aunt Eli who passed away after battling cancer. She was the inspiration for my sijo. She was the kindest and most honest person I will ever know. We knew my aunt's cancer had come back the same year we got our new dog. My mother was in complete despair. We needed something that would help us feel better. To honor my aunt, we wanted to name our dog something close to Eli. We were going to go with Emily but then finally settled on Emma. My aunt saw our new dog on video chats and she said she was the cutest thing she had seen. When my aunt passed away, we decided to give our dog her middle name (Eli) to honor her. She will always be missed.

I learned about this competition from my creative writing teacher Ms. Jorgensen. I never heard of this form of poetry and now it's one of my favorites. I didn't do this poem to win the competition; instead, I did the poem to express myself through writing. Thank you.

MARK PETERSON, PROFESSOR EMERITUS OF KOREAN HISTORY AND LITERATURE, BRIGHAM YOUNG UNIVERSITY

One of my favorites from past years—and I have a lot of favorites among these sijo—is the first place winner from 2016, "Emma", by Austin Snell. Austin was one of the many winners taught by Elizabeth Jorgensen in Wisconsin. Elizabeth describes Austin as a boy who was much more interested in shop and sports than in poetry, yet, he had real emotions for a recently-departed aunt. And he wrote of seeing his aunt in the eyes of their new puppy. "She's still here, on four paws." Beautiful.

The Sanctuary

by Bella Dalton-Fenkl, second place 2016

Tiny snow-white egret wading

      through the sea near broken rocks—

How can a being so fragile

      keep balanced despite the waves?

On the beach, not far from the boardwalk,

      there stands only one tough tree.

BELLA DALTON-FENKL, TWELFTH GRADE, POUGHKEEPSIE, NEW YORK

I live in the Hudson Valley in New York. I'm homeschooled and I will be attending Vassar College this fall. I've loved studying sijo and other Asian poetic forms ever since I read *Urban Temple* and my favorite poems are ones about personal experiences in nature. Last year, I was lucky to be in an Asian poetry course at a local university, in which I had to write, among other things, a haiku every day for a month! It definitely strengthened my understanding of poetic forms, including sijo. My English teacher is a wonderful female Buddhist Lama, Ani Depa, who has helped me explore my interest in poetry over many years of study.

"The Sanctuary" is a poem that describes Silver Sands beach in Connecticut. On a day trip last year, I was walking by a boardwalk. The sun was setting, and I had seen a baby egret stumbling through the sea. A few minutes later I saw a small tree growing on the beach. The tree had clearly been buffeted by a storm in the past—half of it was missing, but it was still healthy. I was so impressed by these small yet determined living creatures that I was inspired to write this sijo.

LUCY PARK, EXECUTIVE DIRECTOR, SEJONG CULTURAL SOCIETY

This sijo is notable for its excellent imagery, illustrating the stark contrast between the fragile egret against its surroundings. However, though the egret appears fragile, it withstands the harsh environment—proving it is just as hardy as the tree. For me, Bella's mastery of words evokes a striking image of a beautiful Korean traditional painting. Her diction is highly effective, and her word economy is superb.

Back in New Orleans

by Dante Kirkman, honorable mention 2016

In the South, Grandpa was born. Paper shack house had a dirt floor.

As a kid he drank coffee. Milk for them was too expensive.

They were rich with gospel spirit! In church they sang, and filled their hearts.

DANTE KIRKMAN, EIGHTH GRADE, PALO ALTO, CALIFORNIA

I'm a student, writer, artist, and boxer. My creative work expresses my viewpoint and experience as a Black youth coming of age in twenty-first century America. My work, often on social justice themes, has been published, exhibited and awarded at the state, national, and international level.

I am very interested in folklore and poetry, as these

traditions figure strongly into the oral traditions of the American Black experience. For example, I have made a documentary on the Black lowrider experience in California, and I have written poetry based on the Harlem Renaissance. As a result, I was very excited to learn about the Sejong Cultural Society's contest, because it gave me an opportunity to combine these interests in an unexpected way, and explore a new genre of poetry. The fact that sijo is a poem that is meant as a song really resonates with African-American traditions.

The theme of a better life is a segue to my sijo poem. My inspiration for the sijo poem was my grandfather, who grew up in segregated New Orleans during the Great Depression with nothing but his faith in God and a resolve to make a better life. After serving in WWII in the Philippines, he settled in San Francisco and made a life for his young family in Menlo Park, California, on the red-lined Black side, east of the freeway. He worked as a mailman and raised five children, and now I am honoring his legacy as his grandson, and my older brother is the first to go to college.

On a final note, the Sejong Cultural Society has helped me expand my horizons to learn more about Korean culture, and for this I am grateful. I am also working on an environmental justice project sponsored by Samsung, a Korean company, and it is empowering to realize that the world is only as big or distant as we choose to make it.

LUCY PARK, EXECUTIVE DIRECTOR, SEJONG CULTURAL SOCIETY

This sijo paints a powerful, vivid picture while evoking strong emotions through excellent wordage. With only a few words the poem clearly illustrates the poverty his grandfather endured; the second line succinctly elaborates and reinforces the image created in the first line. This accentuates the twist in the third line, powerfully juxtaposing material poverty and spiritual wealth. For me, this evokes a striking picture of a poverty-stricken congregation singing in a church with their hearts and spirits filled with joy—bringing a smile to my face. I would claim that Dante, even at his young age, has mastered the essence of sijo.

Untitled

by Clint Gersabeck, first place 2017

With glowing white eyes and shining white teeth, the beast sits in silence
Staring, like a hungry caged dog, demanding to be fed
Nothing is worse than the malevolent glare of a blank page

CLINT GERSABECK, NINTH GRADE, GOLDEN, COLORADO

I am a freshman at D'Evelyn High School. My history teacher, Mrs. Holland, told the class about this competition and encouraged us to submit a sijo poem to the competition. She did a very good job of teaching us to write sijo poetry.

This poem was inspired when I had to write a sijo in history class and could not think of anything to write about. While I was looking at the blank page, Mrs. Holland saw that I had not written anything and jokingly suggested that I write about a blank page. I decided to use this idea and submitted my poem. I would like to thank Mrs. Holland for encouraging me to write my poem and the Sejong Cultural Society for giving me this award.

CHUCK NEWELL, ENGLISH TEACHER AT NOTRE DAME HIGH SCHOOL, CHATTANOOGA, TENNESSEE

I always use this poem as a sample when I am teaching my students to write sijo. It begins with a strong image, and I always tell my students that good poetry is based on imagery. The first line does a great job of establishing the theme, and the second line expands on that theme with another strong image. These are traits of a good sijo. And because the poem does not have a title, the reader is always surprised by the poet's revelation in the final line. That "shock" at the twist makes for an effective sijo, as well. But beyond just following proper sijo form, this poem also expresses a universal truth that every writer goes through, the anxiety of the blank page. The poem doesn't just contain clever irony. It expresses an idea everyone can relate to.

Untitled

by Aidan Boyle, second place 2017

Fiery, spewing lava melting everything away

A volcano rapidly roaring on this cold winter day

How that marshmallow feels in the hot chocolate, I can't say.

AIDAN BOYLE, NINTH GRADE, LITTLETON, COLORADO

I love to play soccer and basketball. I played for my high school (D'Evelyn High School) JV soccer team this year and it was truly a blast. I did not try out for my school's basketball team but I love playing it with my friends. I hope to one day become a mechanical or chemical engineer because I love science and math.

My teacher, Mrs. Holland, told the class about this competition and encouraged all of us to write a poem and submit it in the competition. She taught us the basic format but let us use our creativity to create a meaningful poem that was powerful to each individual person.

The poem I wrote was written in my history class. I was sitting in class on a cold January morning, thinking of something to write my poem about. I thought of the things I loved from sports, to food, but finally winter popped into my head and I knew there had to be something in winter that I could write about. I decided on hot chocolate but had to think of something like it—a volcano! I wrote the poem, turned it in, and won second place. I am honored to receive this award and I would like to thank Mrs. Holland for pushing me to write the poem and the Sejong Cultural Society for this great opportunity.

DEBORAH HOLLAND, HISTORY AND AP PSYCHOLOGY TEACHER AT D'EVELYN HIGH SCHOOL, DENVER, COLORADO

When I first read this sijo, I laughed out loud; the quintessential sijo twist at the end is very satisfying. In my mind, I see a young child coming inside after playing in the cold, winter snow. With red cheeks, the child warms up over a mug of hot chocolate, cradling the mug in their hands, delighted over the marshmallows in the cup. The imagery this sijo provides is vivid and alluring.

I teach this particular sijo to my students every year, and even after reading this sijo many times, the poem still makes me happy. This sijo is very teachable and reachable to my students. Many students are afraid to write poetry, but sijo is different. With sijo, poetry is accessible to all my students, not just the ones who are good at poetry. Students can relate to this sijo as it is about everyday life, which brings it home. I think that students are more willing to try their hand at writing sijo after reading this poem.

Season That Never Comes

by Bryce Toussaint, honorable mention 2018

I lace up stiff metal cleats,

jog yellow foul pole to foul pole,

strap on rugged batting gloves,

and take ground balls off the infield turf.

But it's still minus four outside—

forty two days till first pitch.

BRYCE TOUSSAINT, TWELFTH GRADE, OCONOMOWOC, WISCONSIN

I am seventeen years old and I attend Arrowhead Union High School. My creative writing teacher, Ms. Jorgensen, introduced me to sijo poems. Instantly, my brain was filled with inspiration and ideas, but one stood out. I knew I had to write about baseball because it has been my passion since I could walk. I play on my high school varsity team and I'm continuing my baseball career in college. In college, I plan to get my degree in the medical field to be an athletic trainer or a physical therapist. I like this career because it will keep me involved in sports even after I cannot play.

Being selected as a winner, out of a large number of people who entered this competition, is a tremendous accomplishment. I am very thankful to be named an honorable mention. I would like to thank Ms. Jorgensen because she inspired me to write even when I was not very interested in it, but I could not be happier that she did.

ELIZABETH JORGENSEN, AUTHOR AND HIGH SCHOOL ENGLISH TEACHER

In "Season That Never Comes," my former student Bryce Toussaint used Jackie Robinson as his inspiration. Although this may not be obvious to readers, Bryce told me he used Robinson's number (42) as a metaphor. Bryce said he wanted to allude to what froze Robinson's progress and what prevented Black players from achieving their dreams. I appreciate how even without fully knowing what Toussaint references in "Season That Never Comes", readers can connect with the narrator's longing, persistence, and commitment.

The website History.com offers this information on the

legendary Black baseball player Jackie Robinson:

On April 15, 1947, Jackie Robinson, age 28, becomes the first African American player in Major League Baseball when he steps onto Ebbets Field in Brooklyn to compete for the Brooklyn Dodgers. Robinson broke the color barrier in a sport that had been segregated for more than 50 years. Exactly 50 years later, on April 15, 1997, Robinson's groundbreaking career was honored and his uniform number, 42, was retired from Major League Baseball by Commissioner Bud Selig in a ceremony attended by over 50,000 fans at New York City's Shea Stadium. Robinson's was the first-ever number retired by all teams in the league (History.com).

Belated Breakfast

by Toni Smith, honorable mention 2018

One cup of coffee ready to pour.

Two pieces of wheat toast to eat.

Three spreads of grape jelly.

Four minutes to get ready.

Cat steals my toast, then spills my coffee.

Now, I'm five minutes late.

TONI SMITH, ELEVENTH GRADE, HARTLAND, WISCONSIN

I am a junior at Arrowhead High School. My future goal is to go to Waukesha County Technical College for art and design. My personal interests include being in nature and studying plants and wildlife. I heard about the sijo competition in creative writing class from my teachers, Ms. Jorgensen and Mrs. Hamilton. While writing my sijo poem, I learned how to use rhythm within writing and poetry.

ELIZABETH JORGENSEN, AUTHOR AND HIGH SCHOOL ENGLISH TEACHER

In "Belated Breakfast", Toni Smith references a mundane morning routine gone awry. In the fifth line, Smith cleverly shifts her pattern and flips the plot. I enjoy sharing this sijo with my high school students because it inspires them to consider how cleverness and structure (beyond the syllable groupings) can be used in their own poems. It also helps them understand how life can inspire art.

Abandoned

by Lily Daniels, first place (adult division) 2019

This window reveals mysteries.

  Behind glass, a life that would have been.

As I fade from your memory,

  You grow clearer in my mirror.

Mom, Dad, do you search each other's faces

  For the girl you threw away?

LILY DANIELS, CHESAPEAKE, VIRGINIA

I am currently majoring in English at Old Dominion University with an emphasis in professional writing and minoring in Chinese studies. For the past three years, I have fenced at Tidewater Fencing Club, and my other hobbies include camping, hiking, knitting, and reading.

I learned about this competition through a flier hanging on a wall in the ODU English Department. While I enjoy reading and writing poetry, this was the first time I had encountered sijo. I learned a lot about Korean culture and writing sijo from this experience. My favorite part about writing sijo is the flexibility and creativity within the rules. I am thankful to the Sejong Cultural Society for holding the writing competition and increasing awareness about Korean culture.

The inspiration for my sijo comes from my personal experience. I was left outside of a Family Planning Commission building in China when I was one week old. Even though I love my adoptive family and remember nothing about my first year, it was difficult for me to come to terms with being adopted. There are so many unanswerable questions about my past. Writing is one of the ways I wrestle with these questions and grow from my experiences. I hope that by sharing my writing others are able to understand and relate to my perspective.

DAVID KROLIKOSKI, ASSISTANT PROFESSOR OF KOREAN LITERATURE, UNIVERSITY OF HAWAI'I AT MĀNOA

"Abandoned" begins with a jolt, its compact, one-word title announcing the seriousness of its subject matter as well as the remarkable firmness of the speaker's voice. In inviting the reader to peer through "*this* window" (emphasis mine), the first line of the poem establishes an immediate sense of intimacy with the speaker, whose conviction compels us to also see "a life that would have been" behind this stationary sheet of glass. Daniels' technique is quite polished. The language feels natural and unforced, but has in fact been carefully calibrated: the alliteration between "mysteries," "memory," and "mirror," for example, signals an emergent connection between these ideas as the story of the poem deepens. Modern poets have often deployed the image of a window in their verse, perhaps the most famous Korean example being Jeong Ji-yong in "Window 1", another poem about the relationship between a parent and a child, although the similarities between it and "Abandoned" end there. Daniels' poem is about the act of looking and the power of interpretation. If the speaker is unsure of what her parents choose to see in the present, her own recollection of the past has only grown more vivid over time, a memory that is summed up in the curtness of the poem's unvarnished final line.

A Kisaeng's Sijo

by Hye In Lee, second place 2019

With the rhythm of the janggu, we dance like magpies,

iridescent and spinning, hoping for freedom from the men

and their hands feeling at our ivory ankles, calves, and thighs.

HYE IN LEE, ELEVENTH GRADE, CRESSKILL, NEW JERSEY

Recently, I've sought to incorporate Korean culture into my poetry and wanted to write from the perspective of a woman in Korean history. I came across the stories of the *kisaeng*, who often dealt with the sijo style, and thought it would be interesting to write a sijo from a *kisaeng*'s perspective. I am grateful to the Sejong Cultural Society for inspiring me to learn more about my Korean culture. When I'm not poring over poetry journals or writing some of my own, I like to play the piano and read philosophy!

ELIZABETH JORGENSEN, AUTHOR AND HIGH SCHOOL ENGLISH TEACHER

I have an affinity for poems of contradiction and conflict; these pieces call me to multiple readings, to discover and unfold nuanced layers. Hye In Lee's "A Kisaeng's Sijo" is a poem I return to, each time discovering a deeper subtlety, a more artful craft—it is a poem I appreciate because it's built on complementary opposites and Korean culture using images of the *kisaeng*, *jang-gu*, magpie, and sijo.

Kisaeng

Kisaeng, female property of the state (owned, trained, and registered) and often chosen as concubines for the elite, led multifaceted lives: they were well-respected artists; part of the lowest class and outcasts, yet also revered; and they were the only women allowed to converse with men of status. *Kisaeng* can be seen as a contradiction: controlled by men, yet also ambassadors for their own independence and art. Korean historians insist that the *kisaeng* is not a prostitute. And conversely, all prostitutes claim they are *kisaeng* (lifting their status, but tarnishing the true *kisaeng*). Scholars suggest the number of *kisaeng* working as prostitutes is exaggerated, yet agree these women (often teenagers) were highly skilled in poetry, dance, music, and art.

Kisaeng wrote and performed sijo that frequently explored pain and valediction, and Hye In Lee mirrors these themes in her sijo. Using "ivory" to describe the women makes me think of an ivory tower—perhaps alluding to the *kisaeng* and the men they entertain. And "iridescent" suggests there are different sides to the women, depending on the viewpoint or viewer.

Jang-gu

The *jang-gu* is a two-sided Korean drum with high and low pitches. Played simultaneously, these contrasts are complementary and historically symbolize men and women coming together. Although the men and women in this poem both hear the same *jang-gu*, they don't experience a similar freedom or class. Opening the poem "With the rhythm of the janggu" encourages the reader to find harmony in the opposing factors; to find consonance in the dissonant.

Magpie

Unofficially, the Korean magpie is a national symbol and officially, the bird of some cities. When magpies and tigers are presented in Korean folk art, they're often a commentary on the power of the powerless. Consider if the powerful men in "A Kisaeng's Sijo" are tigers and the women are magpies; the *kisaeng* dances and the prominent men turn her entertainment to the unspeakable. Another paradox: the *kisaeng*, in spite of being owned by the government and a member of the slave class, owes no sexual favors to the aristocrat.

Each time I read "A Kisaeng's Sijo" I'm struck by the writer's cleverness. Hye In Lee writes about Korean history, a Korean performer, a Korean drum, and a Korean bird—in a Korean form of poetry. She uses yin and yang in a poetry form known for contradiction: the sijo's harmonious syllabic pattern; the dominant vowels; and the complementary first two lines and the contradicting third line with its shift, turn, or twist.

It would feel incomplete to say Hye In Lee is successful because she uses one sentence to tell an emotional story; or because she is thought-provoking, visual, and culturally significant; she does all of these things, and she connects with her readers. It's the image of women, "like magpies, iridescent and spinning," trying to escape the advances of men and yet still give pleasure. It is the duality. Balance in imbalance. Freedom in oppression. A disturbing paradigm.

Masterfully crafted with precise language, this one-sentence sijo allows me to see the women twirling and the men objectifying. To hear the drum's rhythm. To feel the lust and dehumanization.

Lost Letters

by Andy Zhao, first place 2020

A hundred thousand love-filled letters I have written for you.

Tonight, my pen runs dry, trapping my words within my mind.

Why do I still stoke the flame that I know will never warm me?

ANDY ZHAO, TWELFTH GRADE, BRITISH COLUMBIA, CANADA

I'm pursuing post-secondary education in computer science, but writing and other creative pursuits have been hobbies of mine for quite a while. Writing poetry, whether structured or free verse, have always been a great expressive and emotional outlet. I feel especially satisfied when my outbursts create something eloquent. I learned about this contest through my creative writing teacher at school. During our poetry unit, she encouraged us to try this type of poetry, and when I first read a contemporary sijo, I was inspired by how much emotion was conveyed with so few words. I felt compelled to submit into this competition—no harm, right? I had no expectations to win, rather, it was just a fun experience. My poem was partly inspired by my own feelings, and partly created in my imagination. I wanted to convey the emotion of desperation and sorrow, and so I just started writing and letting words flow. Love is a complicated thing, and sometimes it's better to think less than to overthink it. I'm honoured to have received the first place award. I entered the competition expecting nothing but a bit of fun, and so I'm honestly in awe that I would be afforded such an honour. To Ms. Smith, thank you for supporting and encouraging me. To the Sejong Cultural Society, thank you for giving me this honour.

MARK PETERSON, PROFESSOR EMERITUS OF KOREAN HISTORY AND LITERATURE, BRIGHAM YOUNG UNIVERSITY

Andy Zhao captures the frustrations and the disappointments of young love in his poem "Lost Letters". He offers two wonderful phrases: "my pen runs dry, trapping my words within my mind." Ah! What a great idea—darned pen! I've written so much that it has run dry! Oh dear. Trapping words in my mind that cannot get out now. Wow! And then, "Why do I stoke the flame that I know will never warm me?" What a great expression of the failure of a relationship, realizing it's going nowhere, but not quite ready to recognize it and give up.

Untitled

by Alice Davidson, first place (adult division) 2020

That sweater, so warm and soft-yet full of holes, hangs unworn.

"Let's toss it!" Downsizing means tough decisions. "No one wears it."

"Wait!" I cry. "Grandma made that when I was young. It still fits."

ALICE DAVIDSON, HOUSTON, TEXAS

I have been a world history and Chinese and East Asian cultures teacher for forty years, the last thirty at Episcopal High School in Houston, Texas. My hobbies include traveling and reading historical fiction, biographies, and anything about Asia. I was fortunate to live in China for several years, and to travel to Korea with the National Consortium for Teaching about Asia in 2017. I learned about sijo while attending the

National Korean Studies Seminar in Los Angeles in 2019. My future goals are to continue finding ways to bring East Asia into my curriculum and provide my students with cross-cultural experiences. My personal hero is my grandmother Alice, for whom I am named. My main childhood memories are of her sitting in a chair knitting and telling stories of past generations of our family.

MARK PETERSON, PROFESSOR EMERITUS OF KOREAN HISTORY AND LITERATURE, BRIGHAM YOUNG UNIVERSITY

The poem is untitled, but it's crying out to be named, "The Sweater". The poem is sentimentality personified. An old, worn-out, hole-filled sweater, but it was knitted by "my grandmother"—I can't throw it away. But the clincher is, "it still fits"—which I think is self-delusional if not an out-and-out lie. There's no way that it still fits, but we want to keep this sentimental work of "my grandmother" so we tell ourselves that "it still fits." Wonderful.

Social Distancing

by Julie Shute, third place (adult division) 2020

Neighborhoods, bereft of neighbors. Teeming cities, bare.

We orbit our own lives. Joined in isolation. All, alone.

We see how our fates are interwoven, just as they unravel.

JULIE SHUTE, ENCINO, CALIFORNIA

I am a middle school teacher from southern California, who enjoys eating good food, traveling, singing in the car, and petting fluffy animals. I was teaching my students about ancient Korea, and was lucky enough to find numerous great sources of information, including the Sejong Cultural Society. I learned about sijo poetry and shared what I'd learned with my kids. I encouraged my students to enter the contest, and was inspired by their creativity to create a poem of my own.

NICK CHIARKAS, AUTHOR OF THE AWARD-WINNING NOVEL *WEEPERS*

"Social Distancing" by Julie Shute is in the moment, and yet it pulls you into its flow. What may at first appear contradictory becomes the rhythm of beauty. It is powerful without being overbearing and gentle without being timid. It is both uplifting and brokenhearted. And it ends with a "pow" and an "ahh." Brilliant. I love this sijo.

Coming home

by Trace Morrissey, honorable mention 2020

Air felt lighter, food tasted better, music more upbeat, sun brighter.

Not seeing my brother in two years, I remained eager.

But he came home in a plane, in a pine box, covered in a flag.

TRACE MORRISSEY, TWELFTH GRADE, HARTLAND, WISCONSIN

I am enlisting in the Air Force with the end goal of becoming a pilot. During my free time, I like to spend time outdoors with friends. I also enjoy going up north to spend time on a lake, or skiing. One person who has always been my hero is my grandpa. He taught me so much about life and how to treat people respectfully. Although we lost him in November 2019, I feel as if he is still teaching me lessons today. I learned, while writing my sijo, I needed to connect with the reader and to trigger an emotion. Since I have learned this, my writing has drastically improved. My inspiration for writing this poem came from a Vietnam War veteran that came and spoke with our class one day. He talked about how he lost good friends in the war and how he cannot forget some of the things he saw while fighting. We also wrote letters in class to veterans going on the Honor Flight. Most people wrote back and those who did had an impact on everyone who read their response.

SEONG-KON KIM, PROFESSOR EMERITUS AT SEOUL NATIONAL UNIVERSITY, VISITING SCHOLAR AT DARTMOUTH COLLEGE, AND AWARD-WINNING LITERARY CRITIC, TRANSLATOR, AND SIJO POET

Marked by heightened poetic sensibility and lyricism, sijo has always been an excellent medium of conveying the poet's innermost feelings and epiphanies of truth. With its pastoral and social themes, sijo can also be a profound insight into nature and a powerful criticism of contemporary society.

"Coming home" is a heartrending sijo poem about the tragic homecoming of the narrator's brother, who has fallen during his military service for the country. The first line is full of life and hope: "Air felt lighter, food tasted better, music more upbeat, sun brighter." In such a buoyant good mood, the narrator is eager to see his brother who is coming home presumably from his tour in a hostile foreign country. Sadly, however, he comes back home in a casket covered with a flag. There is neither fanfare nor a welcoming party for the veteran. Only the narrator's silent tears and heartbreaking sorrow greet his homecoming.

The third line, "But he came home in a plane, in a pine box, covered in a flag" is dry and succinct. Nevertheless, it beautifully renders the poet's intricate sense of loss and bereavement without emotional overflow. Although his homecoming is treated with the utmost care and dignity, and his funeral deserves full military honors, the narrator's brother no longer exists physically. Therefore, nothing can heal the poet's psychic wound or solace his troubled soul drenched by eternal grief.

"Coming home" is a powerful sijo poem that makes us ponder the sorrow of losing someone we dearly love and burying him or her in our hearts. At the same time, the poem subtly suggests that we eventually overcome our sorrow in order to survive and thrive. Life is full of vicissitudes and unfairness. Oftentimes, death takes our beloved ones and other times, we lose our precious things. Still, however, we must deal with it and move on. "Coming home" enlightens us that we may be alone in this world, but we do not need to be lonely.

In Middle School

by Esther Kim, honorable mention 2020

I thought that beauty meant

       discarding my Korean self.

I wished to leave my yellow skin,

       but my umma comforted me;

she said, "Yellow is the color

       of forsythias, bright and beautiful."

ESTHER KIM, ELEVENTH GRADE, POTOMAC, MARYLAND

As a first-generation Korean American, I frequently reflected on my parents' journey to America and their cultural influence on me. This sparked a defined interest at the intersection of English and history, which led to my discovery of poetry. My poems, including the one recognized by the Sejong Cultural Society, often explore my relationships with Korea and America. I am extremely grateful for the efforts of the Sejong Cultural Society in broadening awareness of Korean culture. Through this competition, I have been able to learn about not only the craft of writing sijo but also the often-neglected history of Korea.

SEONG-KON KIM, PROFESSOR EMERITUS AT SEOUL NATIONAL UNIVERSITY, VISITING SCHOLAR AT DARTMOUTH COLLEGE, AND AWARD-WINNING LITERARY CRITIC, TRANSLATOR, AND SIJO POET

"In Middle School" touches upon a painful, compelling identity crisis that Asian immigrants in the U.S. inevitably come to experience in their vulnerable adolescent years. "In Middle School" painstakingly depicts the psychological conflicts of a minority teenage girl who finds that she is different from others. Situated on the border of her home country and host country, the Korean American girl wants to assimilate into the mainstream American society by discarding her differences. Hence, the first line is, "I thought that beauty meant/ discarding my Korean self." Then comes the second line, "I wished to leave my yellow skin,/ but my umma comforted me." Here, she deliberately chooses the Korean word, "umma" instead of "mom," intricately acknowledging the importance of her Korean heritage.

In fact, you do not need to leave your skin color or discard your Korean self. Instead, you can embrace it, be confident in it, and make the most of it. Ethnic or cultural differences have nothing to do with better or worse, or right or wrong. They have to do with variety and diversity. Thus, the girl realizes that her uniqueness and difference can certainly be an advantage in a multiethnic, multicultural society such as America. She does not need to discard her Korean self, because beauty lies in her Korean identity or in the combination of the two cultures that she inherited.

In his celebrated novel, *Yellow*, Korean American writer Don Lee has explored the possibilities of what it means to be Asian American by redefining the concepts of difference and identity. He does not perceive diasporic identity as a crisis. Rather, he embraces it as a new possibility. The final line of the above poem echoes Don Lee, "Yellow is the color/ of forsythias, bright and beautiful." The poet seems to have accepted her mom's advice and overcome her identity crisis already because she has entitled her poem "In Middle School".

The late Edward W. Said, a Palestinian American literary critic, called himself "a self-appointed exile." Despite being an exile on foreign soil, Said seldom grieved or harbored grudges. On the contrary, in his monumental book, *Culture and Imperialism*, Professor Said enlightens us: "Yet when I say exile, I do not mean something sad or deprived. On the contrary, belonging, as it were, to both sides of the imperial divide enables you to understand them more easily."

"In Middle School" reminds me of Edward W. Said who must have had the same identity crisis as a spiritual exile in America. Indeed, it would be nice if Korean American teenagers, too, could have the same confidence and open-mindedness that Edward W. Said had. It is encouraging that Korean sijo is being revived in America, thanks to the strenuous efforts of Dr. David McCann, Dr. Mark Peterson and Dr. Lucy Park. Through sijo, Koreans and Americans can surely understand each other better.

but today, I hear

by Hannah Kim, honorable mention (adult division) 2020

"Did you eat?" Dad asks again,

picking me up from the airport.

I grew up wishing he'd say

"I love you"

like my friends' dads did

but today,

I hear his question as his way of

saying that.

HANNAH KIM, SAN MATEO, CALIFORNIA

I am a philosophy Ph.D. candidate at Stanford University. I'm grateful for the competition and the opportunity it gave me to learn about sijo as a poetic form.

ROBERT YUNE, AUTHOR, POET, AND EDUCATOR

What I love most about sijo—and poetry in general—is the way poems invite a connection. Some curl inward, coyly posing questions, and some poems reach out, beckoning to the reader. In some sijo, mountain vistas and circling birds offer stillness or wisdom that ripples outward. In others, a connection arises from a speaker's observation or unexpected interplay with the landscape.

In "but today, I hear" Hannah Kim presents a neutral, modern setting and a single line of dialogue. Despite the lack of wildlife, color, and flashy literary techniques, her sijo has a graceful sense of movement as she conjures and resolves a specific emotional void. She also evokes longing—one can practically imagine its long echo through the years. I love how, by the end, the speaker of the poem fills this void through an act of translation—as it turns out, her father was saying "I love you" all along.

I'm always impressed by poems that are simultaneously personal and universal. I'm sure many Asian Americans can relate to this sijo's depiction of generational divides and homecoming. At the same time, I suspect anyone with parents—or anyone who's struggled to understand someone else—can easily find a foothold in this poem's emotional terrain.

CHRISTINE HYUNG-OAK LEE, AUTHOR OF *TELL ME EVERYTHING YOU DON'T REMEMBER*

I related strongly to Hannah Kim's sijo in which she unpacks the phrase "Did you eat?" into "I love you". It examines language and culture and her own growth over time in understanding her father, which is to say generations and diaspora, in a succinct and artful manner. I wish this was the sijo that existed when I was growing up.

Nature Walk

by Jeffrey Bolognese, honorable mention (adult division) 2020

We watch the fox, the dog and I, loping along the wooded path.
We pause our stroll, she stops as well, sitting down to regard us.
Then, bored with local wildlife, she turns around and heads for home.

JEFFERY BOLOGNESE, COLUMBIA, MARYLAND

I'm an aerospace engineer at NASA Goddard Space Flight Center. I live in Columbia, Maryland, with my wife Cindy, my son, Nathan, my daughter, Evie, and our husky/golden retriever mixed breed dog, Sadie (and Trident, the turtle and Phantom, the hamster). I became interested in sijo poetry several years ago after hearing a piece about this particular poetry form on KBS World Radio. I've been writing sijo on and off ever since. I've always enjoyed creative writing and, as an engineer, I like the challenge of fitting verse to the specific structure of sijo while still maintaining a song-like quality and ending twist that characterize it. In my free time I enjoy cooking, hiking, playing board games with my family, and trying to play the guitar. My family is very patient with both my cooking and guitar playing!

TRACY KAMINER, RETIRED ENGLISH TEACHER NEAR CHARLOTTESVILLE, VIRGINIA

"Nature Walk" is a snapshot of my life. I spend hours in the woods, photographing birds and the occasional bear, fox, or whatever I find. I often have the sensation of being watched or studied by those I'm seeking. The poem starts with the ambiguous title "Nature Walk". The speaker and the dog may be out for a stroll, but the twist at the end makes it clear that this is the fox's journey, too. There is a loping rhythm to the poem, with short phrases of four syllables starting the first two lines followed by a phrase of seven or eight syllables. The third line starts with a transition "Then" and the longer phrase "bored with local wildlife" changes the pattern of short phrases to long and represents the twist as the fox determines that the nature walk is over. I can relate to this moment where the observer becomes the observed. As a bird sounds a warning and darts behind a tree or a deer watches and waits before she snorts and leaps away, I am regularly reminded that I am only one being moving through this beautiful creation.

Works Cited

"Jackie Robinson Breaks Color Barrier." *History.com*, A&E Television Networks, www.history.com/this-day-in-history/jackie-robinson-breaks-color-barrier.

Contributors

Deborah Holland is a history teacher at D'Evelyn High School in the Denver metro area, and has also taught in Arizona and Venezuela. She currently teaches Eastern Civilizations, which includes a three-week unit on Korea, and AP Psychology. She first learned about sijo at the 2014 Korean Academy for Educators Seminar in Los Angeles and has taught it ever since. She has shared her enthusiasm of sijo by teaching other educators about the poetry at an NCTA workshop, a Korean War Legacy workshop, and at the National Council of Social Studies. Besides her work with the Sejong Cultural Society, she is a teacher fellow with Qatar Foundation International, which promotes education about the Middle East, as well as with the Engaging Eurasia Teacher Fellowship through Harvard.

Elizabeth Jorgensen is a writer and teacher. She has presented on sijo at a variety of conferences, including National Council of Teachers of English, Wisconsin State Reading Association, Wisconsin Writers Association, and elsewhere. Her articles on sijo have been published in *English Journal, Azalea, Edutopia, Teachers & Writers Magazine,* and *Whale Road Review*, among others. Jorgensen has received numerous awards, including Carroll University's Graduate of the Last Decade, Arrowhead Union High School's teacher of the year, and The Henry Ford's Innovation Nation Teacher Innovator Award. She was a Lucille S. Pooley Award winner (for Successful Techniques in Teaching Composition in the Schools of Wisconsin) and the Jarvis E. Bush winner from the Wisconsin Council of Teachers of English. Learn more on her website: lizjorgensen.weebly.com

Tracy Kaminer is a retired English teacher who has taught at Marist School in Atlanta and Randolph-Macon Academy in Front Royal, Virginia. She specialized in teaching world literature in high school and at community colleges. She also taught ESL in Egypt and in the US. Now she and her husband live near Charlottesville, Virginia, and she works part time in undergraduate admissions for the University of Virginia.

Seong-Kon Kim is a professor emeritus of Seoul National University and a visiting scholar at Dartmouth College. From 2012 to 2017, Kim was President of the Literary Translation Institute of Korea (a ministerial appointment with the Government of the Republic of Korea). On May 19, 2017, Kim received an Honorary Doctorate of Humane Letters from the State University of New York "in recognition of the profound impact Professor Kim has had as a cultural and literary bridge between Korea and the United States."

Professor Kim received his Ph.D. in English from SUNY/Buffalo under Professor Leslie A. Fiedler and studied comparative literature at Columbia University under Professor Edward W. Said. Professor Kim has received, among others, the SUNY/Buffalo Internationally Distinguished Alumni Award, CU Distinguished Alumnus Award, and the Fulbright Distinguished Alumnus Award.

He was the founding president of the Korean Association of Literature and Film from 1998 to 2001, and was president of the International Association of Comparative Korean Studies from 2001 to 2003, president of the Korean Association of Modern Fiction in English from 2004 to 2006, and president of the American Studies Association of Korea from 2007 to 2008. Kim was chairman of the Development and Promotion Council of the English Language and Literature Association of Korea from 2004 to 2005.

A prizewinning literary critic, Kim initiated the debate on literary postmodernism for the first time in Korea in the late 1970s and early 1980s. He was also a pioneer in postcolonialism and cultural studies in Korea. His books on postmodernism, postcolonialism, and cultural studies have greatly influenced Korean writers and scholars. In 2008, Kim received the prestigious Kim Hwantae Award for Literary Criticism and in 2014 the Woo Ho Humanities Award.

Kim was the editor of literary journals such as *Literature & Thought, 21st Century Literature, Contemporary World Literature* and *Korea Journal*. In addition, Kim has been a regularly featured columnist for the *Korea Herald* since 2003. His *Herald* columns have frequently appeared in international media such as *The Nation, The China Post, AsiaOne, Pakistan Observer, The Star, Yahoo! News, The Straits Times, The Kathmandu Post, The Statesman, The World Weekly* and others. He served as co-editor of *Korea Journal* published by the Korean National Commission for UNESCO for 2015-2016. Kim was appointed as head judge of the prestigious Ho-am Prize Selection Committee, a Korean version of the Nobel Prize, and also the Segye Ilbo Literary Prize. Presently, he is a judge for two prestigious literary awards: the Yi Sang Literary Award and the Park Kyungni Literary Prize.

Wonsook Kim (Artist) was born in 1953 in Busan, Korea. She began drawing at a young age. Some of her earliest influences came from Korean folk stories and Christian Bible stories. She studied traditions of art in high school and college in Korea, and graduated with a B.S. and Master of Fine Arts degree from Illinois State University in 1978. After graduation, she moved to New York City to pursue a career as a painter and exhibiting artist.

Kim is renowned for the symbolic narratives reflected in her drawings, prints, paintings, sculptures, and books. Kim's artworks are the result of her lifetime experiences in Korea and the United States, and have been shown in over sixty solo exhibitions around the world. She was awarded an honorary Doctor of Arts degree to recognize her artistic achievements during Illinois State University's Founders Day on February 21, 2019.

Illinois State University's College of Fine Arts and the School of Art was named the Wonsook Kim College of Fine Arts and the Wonsook Kim School of Art on September 12, 2019, in recognition of Kim's generosity to her alma mater. She is married to Thomas Park Clement, a Korean-American adoptee, who is a medical device inventor and entrepreneur.

David McCann taught Korean literature at Harvard University until his retirement in 2014. He particularly enjoyed teaching his class Writing Asian Poetry, a creative writing class exploring the Classical Chinese, Japanese haiku, and Korean sijo forms for English-language poetry. His more recent books include *Urban Temple*, a collection of his English-language sijo poems from Bo-Leaf Press in 2010, published in a dual-language, Korean and English edition by Changbi Publishers in Seoul in 2012; *Slipping Away*, a Korean p'ansori-style narrative poem from Finishing Line Press, a chapbook published in 2013; and *Same Bird*, new and selected poems from Moon Pie Press in 2016. One of his haiku poems published in *Acorn* haiku journal received The Haiku Foundation Touchstone Award in 2014 and is included in Haiku 2015, from Modern Haiku Press. McCann translated the poems included in the collection *The Temple of Words: An Anthology of Modern Korean Buddhist Poetry* published by the Jogye Order of Korean Buddhism, Seoul, in 2017.

Chuck Newell is an English teacher at Notre Dame High School and an award-winning sijo poet. He has taught sijo writing for the past nine years. He first became interested in Korea and Korean poetry because of the many Korean students who have attended his high school over the years. He has attended many seminars about Korean culture and has even traveled to Korea. He has three adult children and lives with his wife and two cats in Chattanooga, Tennessee. His cats are often the subject of his poetry.

Linda Sue Park is the author of many books for young readers, including the 2002 Newbery Medal winner *A Single Shard* and the New York Times bestseller *A Long Walk to Water*. Her most recent titles are *The One Thing You'd Save*, a novel-in-verse, *Prairie Lotus*, a historical fiction middle-grade novel, and *Gurple and Preen*, a picture book. When she's not writing, speaking, teaching, or caregiving for her two grandchildren, she spends most of her time on equity/inclusion work for We Need Diverse Books and the Society of Children's Books Writers and Illustrators. She is also on the advisory board of The Rabbit hOle national children's literature museum project.

Linda Sue has served as a panelist for several awards and grants, including the Kirkus Prize, the National Book Award, the PEN Naylor grant, and the SCBWI Golden Kite Award. In her travels to promote reading and writing, she has visited more than thirty countries and forty-nine states. Linda Sue Park knows very well that she will never be able to read every great book ever written, but she keeps trying anyway.

Lucy Park is one of the founding members of the Sejong Cultural Society, a non-profit organization founded in 2004. As Executive Director, she oversees all programs including the Sejong Music Competition, Sejong Writing Competition, and sijo education programs. She has been very active in teaching about sijo to teachers, students, and adults throughout the US for over ten years. She developed and compiled extensive reference materials on the basics of English sijo writing, sijo samples, and teaching sijo on the Sejong Cultural Society's website and YouTube Channel. She pioneered the Sejong Cultural Society's Sijo and Music program, organizing concerts and commissioning composers and songwriters to write sijo music in a variety of musical genres.

Dr. Park has been a faculty member of the University of Illinois at Chicago College of Medicine for over thirty years. She specializes in pediatric allergy, immunology, and pulmonology and received her M.D. from Seoul National University in Korea.

Mark Peterson (professor emeritus of Korean history, literature and language, Department of Asian and Near Eastern Languages. Brigham Young University, Provo, UT) received B.A. in Asian Studies and Anthropology from Brigham Young University in 1971. He received his M.A. in 1973 and his Ph.D. in 1987, both from Harvard University in the field of East Asian Languages and Civilization. Prior to coming to BYU in 1984 he was the director of the Fulbright program in Korea from 1978 to 1983. He has been the coordinator of the Asian Studies Program and was the director of the undergraduate programs in the David M. Kennedy Center for International Studies. Dr. Peterson is a member of the Association for Asian Studies, where he was formerly the chair of the Korean Studies Committee; was also the book review editor for *The Journal of Asian Studies* for Korean Studies books. He is also a member of the Royal Asiatic Society, the International Association for Korean Language Education, the International Korean Literature Association, and the American Association of Korean Teachers. He served as past editor-in-chief for the *Korea Journal*, published by UNESCO in Korea, from 2015 to 2017. Currently he is working with a research center he founded called The Frog Outside the Well Research Center, which publishes an active YouTube channel by that name. He also writes a weekly column for *The Korea Times*.

Seo, Kwan-ho and is the founder and publisher of *Children's Sijo World* (어린이 시조나라) magazine. Seo has published seven anthologies of sijo for children and received numerous accolades as a poet, educator and publisher. He is a dedicated educator who has taught sijo to children for several decades. Seo has also presented at workshops where he coaches educators in how to teach sijo to children.

Index of Poems

Poets

First Line

Title

References

The following is a list of books and links in English that will serve as a reference in learning about sijo, literature, history and culture of Korea.

Azalea: Journal of Korean Literature and Culture. Young-Jun Lee, Editor-in-Chief. Korea Institute, Harvard University, University of Hawaii Press, 2011-2020.

Brous, Kathy. "Lyric song and the birth of the Korean nation" in *Korean Art Songs: An Anthology and Guide* by Moon-Sook Park, You-Seon Kim Vol 1., Classical Vocal Reprints, 2017.

Cho, Oh-hyun. *For Nirvana: 108 Zen Sijo Poems.* New York, Columbia University Press, 2016.

Chon, Young-Ae. *Im Lied Jedoch-in globalisierten Welt. Reiner Kunzes Korea-Gedichte.*

Chon, Young-Ae: *Grenzgänge der poetischen Sprache.* Würzburg 2013 (in German).

Connor, Mary. *The Koreas (Nations in Focus).* ABC-CLIO, 2009.

Connor, Mary. *Teaching East Asia: Korea. Lessons and Resources for K-12 Classrooms* (e-book). National Korean Studies Seminar, 2019. https://koreanseminar.org/teachingeast/

Contogenis, Constantine, Wolhee Choe. *Hwang Jini & Other Courtesan Poets from the Last Korean Dynasty.* Hawks Publishing, New York, 2006.

Cummings, Bruce. *Korea's Place In the Sun, A Modern history.* W. W. Norton & Company. New York, 2005.

Gendrano, Victor P. *Rustle of Bamboo Leaves. Selected Haiku and Other Poems.* Morrisville, North Carolina, Lulu Enterprises, Inc. 2005.

Gross, Larry. *Asian Poetry: The Korean Sijo.*
https://thewordshop.tripod.com/Sijo/sijo-index.htm

Gross, Larry. *Sijo Masters in Translation.*
thewordshop.tripod.com/Sijo/masters.html

Gross, Larry and Elizabeth St. Jacques. *Sijo West, Journal of North American Sijo*. Vol.1-2, Tallahassee Florida, 1996-1998.

Higginson, William and Penny Harter. *The Haiku Handbook: How to Write, Share, and Teach Haiku*. Tokyo, Kodansha International, 1985.

Holland, Deb and Lucy Park. Holland: Teaching Sijo. Google Slide Presentation. Denver, Colorado, 2020.
https://bit.ly/3AnYw8g

Kim, Gi-soo. *Korean Musicology Series. Series 10. Gagok, Gasa, Sijo. Danga, gin-japga*. Music Score (국악전집 10, 정간보:), National Gukak Center.

Kim, Jaihiun. *Master Sijo Poems from Korea: Classical and Modern.* Si-sa-yong-o-sa Publishers, Seoul, 1982.

Kim, Jaihiun. *Classical Korean Poetry*. Fremont, California, Asian Humanities Press, 1994.

Kim, Jaihiun. *Modern Korean Verse in Sijo Form*. Vancouver, BC, Ronsdale Press, 1997.

Kim, Min-jeong. *Going Together*. Goyoachim Publishers, 2020.

Kim, Unsong. *Classical Korean Poems (Sijo): Selected and translated by Kim Unsong. Revised edition.* San Bruno California, One Mind Press, 1987.

Kim, Unsong. *Poems of Modern Sijo*. California, One Mind Press, 1995.

Kim, Wolha. "Chung-san-li". Sejong Cultural Society.
https://www.youtube.com/watch?v=_Ua6p9S0o8

Korea.net: Culture https://www.korea.net/NewsFocus/Culture

Kwon, Youngmin and Fulton, Bruce. *What is Korean Literature?* Korea Research Monograph 37. University of California, Berkeley Institute of East Asian Studies, 2020. http://ieas.berkeley.edu/publications/

Lee, Peter H. *Anthology of Korean Poetry: From the Earliest Era to the Present*. New York, John Day Publisher, 1964.

Lee, Peter H. *Anthology of Korean Literature. From Early Times to the Nineteenth Century*. University of Hawaii Press, 1981.

Lim, Jae Won. *Korean Musicology Series 9. Gagok, Gasa, Sijo. Classical Vocal Music of Korea* (국악전집#9), The National Gukak Center.

Seoul, 2018.

McCann, David R. *Early Korean Literature: Selections and Introductions.* New York, Columbia Press, 2000.

McCann, David R. *Urban Temple. Sijo, Twisted and Straight.* Bo-Leaf Books, 2008.

Munhak-namu. Summer 2004.

O'Rourke, Kevin. *The Sijo Tradition.* Seoul, Korea, Jung Eum Sa, 1987.

Park, Linda Sue. *Tap Dancing On the Roof.* New York, Houghton Mifflin Harcourt, 2007.

Park, Linda Sue. *The One Thing You'd Save.* Clarion Books, 2021.

Park, Lucy. *Sijo: Structure and Samples.* PowerPoint Slides, 2021. https://www.sejongculturalsociety.org/resources/powerpoint_sijo.html

Rutt, Richard. *The Bamboo Grove: An Introduction to Sijo.* University of Michigan Press, 1998.

St. Jacques, Elizabeth. *Around the Tree of Light.* Ontario, Canada, Maplebud Press, 1995.

St. Jacques, Elizabeth. *In the Light. Sijo.* startag.tripod.com/SijoCont.html

St. Jacques, Elizabeth. *How to Write Linked Sijo and Sijo Sequences*, 1996. http://startag. tripod.com/LinkedSijo.html

Sejong Cultural Society YouTube Channel. https://www.youtube.com/user/KoreanTheme

Sijo Munhak Sajeon #1409.

The Association of Korean History Teachers. *A Korean History for International Readers. What Do Koreans Talk About Their Own History and Culture?* Seoul, Humanist Publishing Group Inc., 2010.

Walker, Tamara, *Fabric Heart: A Collection of Contemporary Introspective Sijo.* Georgetown, Kentucky, Finishing Line Press, 2019.

Watkins, R.W., Ed. *Wholly Trinities: The Nocturnal Iris Anthology of Sijo in English.* Canada, Nocturnal Iris Publications, 2020.

Zong, In-Sob. *Guide to Korean Literature.* Seoul, Hollym Intl. Corp, 1983.

References in Korean

The following is a list of books and links in Korean that will serve as a reference in learning about Korean sijo.

Choe, Nam-seon (최남선). *One Hundred Eight Defilement* (백팔번뇌). Tae Hak Sa Publisher (태학사), Pa-gu, Gyung-gi-do. 2006. (Originally published in 1926).

Im, Jong-chan (임종찬). *Essence of the Ancient Sijo* (고시조의 본질). Gughak Jaryo Won (국학자료원), Seoul 1992.

Im, Jong-chan (임종찬). *Sijo Principles* (시조학원론). Gughak Jaryo Won (국학자료원), Seoul, 2014.

Im, Jong-chan (임종찬). *Potato Flower* (감자꽃). Sejong Publisher (세종출판사), Seoul 2017.

Jang, Sa-hoon (장사훈). *Sijo Music Theory* (시조음악론). Seoul National University Press, Seoul 2006.

Kim, Ghi-soo (김기수). *Anthology of Korean Music.* (국악전집: 가사, 시조, 단가, 긴잡가). National Gugak Center (국립국악원), 1982.

Kim, Haesook (김해숙), Paik Dae-woong, Choi Tai-hyun. *Introduction to Traditional Korean Music* (전통음악개론). Eu-ul-rim Publisher (어울림), Seoul, 1995.

Kim, Jaehyun (김제현). Writing Modern Sijo (현대시조작법). Sae-mun Publisher, Seoul. 1999

Kim, Jung-ja (김정자). *History Lessons in Sijo Poems* (한수의 시조에 역사가 살아있다). Gughak Jaryo Won(국학자료원), Seoul, 2011.

Park, Eul-soo (박을수). *Master Encyclopedia of Korean Sijo* (한국시조대사전) Vol 1 & 2 (상, 하). Asea Munhwa Sa (아세아문화사), Seoul, 1991.

Park, Mi-young (박미영). *Sijo* (시조). from *Encyclopedia of Korean Culture.* Academy of Korean Studies (한국학중앙연구소), 2009.
https://www.youtube.com/watch?v=__Ua6p9S0o8&list=RDEM1tc69yuG

28P20BjmLgL16w&index=2

Seo Kwan-Ho (서관호). *Short Sunflower, An anthology of sijo for children* (키작은 해바라기). Children's Sijo World Publisher, 2011.

Seo Kwan-Ho (서관호). *Sijo even my dog knows* (강아지도 아는 시조). Children's Sijo World Publisher, 2017.

Yi, Yong-ho (이용호). *Modern sijo; research with focus on Choi, Nam-sun; Yi, Eun-sang, Yi, Byong-gi* (근대시조의 재조명 연구. 최남선, 이은상, 이병기의 작품분석을 중심으로). Dong-gwang Moon-hwa publisher (동광문화사), Seoul, 2004.

The
Sejong Cultural Society

www.sejongculturalsociety.org

About the Sejong Cultural Society

The Sejong Cultural Society strives to advance awareness and understanding of Korea's cultural heritage amongst people in the United States by reaching out to the younger generations through contemporary creative and fine arts.

It is our hope that, through this, the rich culture behind Korea's history will be accessible to people of any ethnicity and nationality while being a unique part of Western culture, and that such harmonizing of the two cultures will create a better understanding between them.

The main program includes

1. Sejong Music Competition for piano and violin
   Open to students younger than 18 years in North America
   Contestants are required to perform a piece with Korean theme
2. Sejong Writing Competition
   Open to adults and students in North America
   The essay category: read a short fiction by a Korean author and write an essay in English in response to the prompts
   The sijo category: write a sijo in English on any topic
3. Sejong International Sijo Competition
   Open to poets of all ages and nationality
   Write a sijo in English
4. Sijo Education
   Open to educators, students, and poets
   Virtual or in-person workshops and classes
   Online asynchronous classes

The Sejong Cultural Society is a 501(c)(3) not-for-profit organization.
Visit www.SejongCulturalSociety.org for more information

Publication of this book was supported in part by grants from the Illinois Arts Council, BISCO foundation, and the Oversea Korea Foundation.